Renowned poet Fleur Adcock here provides modern verse translations of the complete work of two of the most exciting poets of the twelfth century, Hugh Primas of Orleans and the so-called Archpoet, beside their Latin originals. Included are witty epigrams, treatments of classical themes, poems on religious and ecclesiastical topics, depictions of low life, begging-poems, and the Archpoet's famous 'Confession'. The work is characterised by its liveliness and its touches of satire and coarse realism, features which Fleur Adcock captures superbly in her modern renderings. There are textual notes, explanatory notes, a historical note, and an introduction. This unique resource will appeal not only to medievalists but to all lovers of poetry.

Cambridge Medieval Classics 2

Hugh Primas and the Archpoet

Cambridge Medieval Classics

General editor

PETER DRONKE, FBA

Professor of Medieval Latin Literature, University of Cambridge

This series is designed to provide bilingual editions of medieval Latin and Greek works of prose, poetry, and drama dating from the period *c.* 350–*c.* 1350. The original texts are offered on left-hand pages, with facing-page versions in lively modern English, newly translated for the series. There are introductions, and explanatory and textual notes.

The Cambridge Medieval Classics series allows access, often for the first time, to outstanding writing of the Middle Ages, with an emphasis on texts that are representative of key literary traditions and which offer penetrating insights into the culture of medieval Europe. Medieval politics, society, humour, and religion are all represented in the range of editions produced here. Students and scholars of the literature, thought, and history of the Middle Ages, as well as more general readers (including those with no knowledge of Latin or Greek) will be attracted by this unique opportunity to read vivid texts of wide interest from the years between the decline of the Roman empire and the rise of vernacular writing.

Opening titles

1 Nine Medieval Latin Plays, translated and edited by PETER DRONKE
2 Hugh Primas and the Archpoet, translated and edited by FLEUR ADCOCK
3 Johannes de Hauvilla, *Architrenius*, translated and edited by WINTHROP WETHERBEE

Other titles in preparation

Prodromic Poems, translated and edited by MARGARET ALEXIOU and MICHAEL HENDY
Adelard of Bath, *Quaestiones Naturales* and *De Eodem et Diverso*, translated and edited by CHARLES BURNETT
Dante, *De Vulgari Eloquentia*, translated and edited by STEVEN BOTTERILL
Dante, *Monarchia*, translated and edited by PRUDENCE JAMES
Digenis Akritas, translated and edited by ELIZABETH JEFFREYS
Nigel of Longchamp, *Speculum Stultorum*, translated and edited by JILL MANN
Dhuoda, *Liber Manualis*, translated and edited by MARCELLE THIÉBAUX
Gregory of Nazianzus, Autobiographical Poems, translated and edited by CAROLINNE WHITE
Peter Abelard, The Theological and Polemical Letters, translated and edited by JEAN ZIOLKOWSKI

Hugh Primas and the Archpoet

TRANSLATED AND EDITED BY
FLEUR ADCOCK

CAMBRIDGE
UNIVERSITY PRESS

Published by the Press Syndicate of the University of Cambridge
The Pitt Building, Trumpington Street, Cambridge CB2 IRP
40 West 20th Street, New York, NY 10011-4211, USA
10 Stamford Road, Oakleigh, Melbourne 3166, Australia

First published 1994

Printed in Great Britain at the University Press, Cambridge

A catalogue record for this book is available from the British Library

Library of Congress cataloguing in publication data
Hugo Primas, Aurelianensis, c. 1093–c. 1160
[Poems. English]
Hugh Primas and the Archpoet / translated and edited by Fleur Adcock
　 p.　cm. – (Cambridge medieval classics: 2)
Includes bibliographical references
ISBN 0 521 39546 1
1. Hugo Primas, Aurelianensis, c. 1093–c. 1160 – Translations into English.
2. Latin poetry, Medieval and modern – Translations into English.
3. Archipoeta, fl. 1140–1165 – Translations into English.
4. Latin poetry, Medieval and modern.　5. Goliards.
I. Archipoeta, fl. 1140–1165. Poems. English. 1994.
II. Adcock, Fleur.　III. Title.　IV. Series.
PA8347.H77A23　1994
881'.02–dc20　93–46136 CIP

ISBN 0521 39546 1 hardback

Acknowledgement

I am most grateful to the British Academy for a grant that met the cost of preparing
electronic copy for this volume from my typescript.

　　　　　　　　　　　　　　　　　　　　　　　　　　　　　　F.A.

CE

Contents

Introduction

Hugh Primas and the Archpoet are the two most notable of the twelfth-century poets known as 'Goliardic'. For centuries both were anonymous. The Archpoet still is, in that he cannot be identified with a nameable historical individual (although many conjectures have been and continue to be made); but there is now general agreement on the corpus of work to be assigned to him and on some details of his life. Primas, however, has been brought out of the shadows and shown to be not some vague appellation for one or more wandering versifiers but the scholar and teacher Hugh Primas of Orléans.

As A. G. Rigg has pointed out in 'Golias and other Pseudonyms', both titles – 'Primas' and 'Archipoeta' – were in medieval times used to some extent interchangeably as labels for the authors of various skilful and witty poems. They were praise-words, not personal names. Rigg's article calls into question the ascription of certain individual poems to Hugh of Orléans, but agrees that there is no reason to doubt his existence.

It was Wilhelm Meyer who convincingly showed Hugh's pre-eminent claim to the title of 'Primas'. He had become curious about the contents of Rawlinson MS G109, as described in the 1895 'Summary Catalogue of Western Manuscripts in the Bodleian Library...', and in 1906 he travelled to Oxford to see it. The opening pages proved to contain a group of twenty-three poems, twelve of them previously unknown, and all of them, he believed, by the same author. Eight of them (poems 1,2,11,15,16,18,21 and 23) were 'internally signed' by the name of Primas, and there was evidence from other sources that four more might well be his. These twenty-three poems now make up the accepted canon of Hugh Primas' work, and my text is based on Meyer's transcription of them in his 1907 edition.

Up to that time, as he so vividly put it, the name Primas had for decades 'walked like a ghost through the literature'. The excitement he derived from reading the Oxford manuscript and discovering what it implied can still be felt. He has been criticised by Rigg and others (including C. J. McDonough, who published the most recent edition of

Primas) for allowing himself to be too easily persuaded by circumstantial evidence; but as a relative amateur in the field I am content to leave such arguments to the scholars. My interest is in the poems themselves.

If Goliardic poetry is to be confined to that which contains elements of satire and deals with such subjects as wine, women, gambling and attacks on the establishment, then the work of Primas transcends the definition, although the traditional subjects are well represented. His poems include plenty of satire and personal invective (against people who have cheated him or treated him brutally, in poems 1,15 and 23; against prostitutes, in 7 and 8; against wicked churchmen and a heretic, in 16 and 18), and sex, wine and gambling are also featured; but in addition there are treatments of classical themes such as Orpheus and Eurydice, Ulysses and the fall of Troy, and an exercise on the biblical story of Dives and Lazarus. In this last, however (poem 5), it is not difficult to discern a parallel – albeit a typically exaggerated one – between the poor man begging for food and Primas himself; just as in poem 3 Orpheus is depicted as begging from Pluto, and in poem 10 the plight of Ulysses, returning to Ithaca with no means of supporting himself after years of wandering, clearly arouses the poet's particular sympathy. Primas has a highly personal approach to his work. His own concerns are dear to him, and he figures regularly as a character in his poems, often by name: in 1,26 it is 'poor Primas' who has lost money; in 16,139 'Primas, who is poor and in need' appeals for charity; 15 positively oozes with self-pity for 'our good poet Primas'. Even his cloak, in 2c, addresses him by name and offers sympathy.

Cloak-poems are a recognised genre. Primas took his inspiration for those he wrote from Martial, who has several epigrams on the subject: in vi,82, for example, he begs Rufus for a good cloak, and in viii,28 he eulogises a new toga he has been given but says that it will make his old cloak look ridiculous. He was the first Latin poet to write true 'begging-poems' and to advertise his poverty shamelessly in his verse – a habit which Primas in his turn adopted and made popular.

The portrait of a whining self-seeker, given to begging for presents or sympathy and complaining about his misfortunes, may not sound immediately appealing; but there is more to be said. For example, I have mentioned exaggeration; this is a customary tool of the satirist, and one of several techniques Primas uses for comic effect. He calculatedly exaggerates his poverty, his age and his frailty, and doesn't hesitate to joke about his short stature, calling himself 'a Zacchaeus' in poem 15. There his assailant is a Judas, a Herod, a Dacian, while Primas himself is an old man at death's door who is nevertheless granted a miraculous turn of speed – 'winged feet' – and flies to safety. Even the form of the poem, with its deliberately repetitive variations on a theme, piles on the effects, managing in the end to be pathetic as well as ridiculous. Poem 16 is full of over-the-top descriptions of excess: the bishop's super-human greed, his 'thousands of thousands' of relations, his ram-like lust. Sometimes the tone is vicious, but there are some pleasantly amusing touches, such as the young aspirant to office in lines 76–7 who would have been prepared to bribe a mule with gold plate. We should also not forget that many of the characters in this and other poems who mean nothing to us, except as material for scholarly speculation, would have been immediately recognisable to Primas' audience; he knew how to raise laughs by topical references.

As for his classical references, many of those in such poems as 14 and 15 would likewise have been picked up by an educated audience, and the themes of poems 3, 9 and 10 were based on subject-matter currently familiar. (See my notes to these poems.) Orléans was a well-known centre for classical learning, in which Primas was thoroughly trained. His expertise in the use of Latin as an instrument for writing verse shines forth in his work.

The mood of the poems varies. In general the work of Primas has been described as darker or more sombre and more vindictive than that of the Archpoet, and his style as cruder. Certainly his language can be coarse, and not only in the traditional sense; in the past poem 8, for instance, gave offence to those who were inclined to be scandalised by sexual explicitness, but elsewhere he uses expressions which are differently offensive: in poem 2A 'a disgusting sore' (*sordida struma*) is strong language when applied to a member of the clergy, and the similar image of ulcers running with pus in poem 5 is even more revolting than in the biblical passage on which it is based. But his vulgarity can be subtle, as it were, involving *double entendres* or suggestiveness: in 8, 47 the prostitute's 'smelly den' is not ostensibly an anatomical reference, and in 1, 33–4 there is word-play in '*turgida culo, evacuata*'. Primas was far from being unsophisticated. His satire can be cruel, but it is often expressed with grace and wit.

An essential element in the effectiveness of his poetry is his facility in rhymed verse-forms. He uses both quantitative metres, such as hex-ameters and elegiac couplets, and rhythmical verse, but there is always rhyme. His favourite form is Leonine verse: hexameters in which the first section of each line, before the caesura, rhymes with the remaining part. These make up poems 2–10, as well as some of the shorter, epigrammatic ones. There is sometimes additional rhyming at the ends of lines as well as internally; for example, in poem 9 the lines rhyme in couplets, with an occasional triplet (lines 27–9, 38–40, 47–9) and one single line at the end rhyming only internally. Poem 1 is in elegiac couplets, with end-rhyme, and this occurs also in 17 and in the first four lines of 14, which ends with two hexameters.

As for the rhythmical poems, his well-known complaint 'Dives eram et dilectus...' (poem 23) uses octosyllabics with large blocks of up to eleven lines rhyming together – the device known as 'tirade rhyme', which gives a particularly powerful impression of angry passion. Poem 18, a somewhat calmer piece, has lines of this length but rhyming mostly in couplets. Poem 15 is something of a hybrid, beginning with hexameters in tirade rhyme but then switching to a pattern of rhythmical strophes, with what Meyer calls Primas' inclination to tirade rhyme dominating the rhyme-scheme. In poem 16 it is the language, rather than the form, which is a hybrid: Latin and French are combined in a poem of mostly twelve-syllable lines, with tirade rhyme tending to take over once again.

Primas' virtuosity in rhyme gave him additional scope for comic effects; absurd or unexpected rhymes can be entertaining in themselves (as in some of Ogden Nash's verse). Poem 2 contains examples of such witty rhyming. But Primas was also capable of a more elevated and dignified style, as in poem 9 with its elegiac tone.

The Archpoet was perhaps a generation younger than Primas (his surviving work dates from the early 1160s, whereas Primas evidently flourished in the 1130s and 40s). All that is definitely known of him comes from the internal evidence of his poems or from what can be deduced about his movements from those of his patron, Rainald of Dassel, Archchancellor to the Emperor Frederick Barbarossa and later Archbishop of Cologne. As W. H. T. Jackson has said (in 'The Politics of a Poet: the Archipoeta as revealed by his imagery'), even his name is 'a mocking travesty of a title', probably a play on that of the Archicancellarius. I shall refrain from reporting on the mass of biographical speculation about the poet (which still continues) except to mention the suggestion of Peter Dronke (in 'The Archpoet and the Classics') that he may well have been at some stage a disciple of Primas at Orléans, where he would have had access to the classical literature of which he shows so extensive a knowledge. As Dronke points out, the Archpoet seems to have been influenced by Primas in his use of certain verse-forms: for example, poem II is in octosyllabics with tirade rhyme, a form used by Primas for 'Dives eram et dilectus'; the two poems have thematic elements in common (in each the poet claims to have been in disgrace), but the Archpoet can be seen as attempting to outdo his predecessor by beginning with sixteen lines, rather than ten, all rhyming perfectly together.

As far as versification is concerned the Archpoet was not an innovator, but simply a superb practitioner of what had already been tried. Like Primas he also used Leonine hexameters (in poem III and the first part of poem VI, of which the second part consists of *caudati*, or end-rhymed hexameters, arranged in quatrains); but his preference on the whole was for rhythmical verse, and in particular the Goliardic measure, or 'Vagantenstrophe', which he deployed so brilliantly in poems IV, V, IX and X. The introduction to Watenphul and Krefeld's edition gives numerous detailed examples of how his vocabulary and syntax were at times influenced by the needs of rhyme: for instance, in I,8,2 he uses the rare word *opilio* for 'shepherd', rather than the more obvious *pastor*, and in poem III he veers between the singular and plural when speaking of himself, according to whether the rhyme requires *me* or *nos*. But poets in any age or language may have recourse to such expedients without compromising the essential naturalness of their style, as long as they observe reasonable limits. The Archpoet seldom seems to have strained unduly for his effects; the adverb *nane*, in poem IV,5,2, is a rare instance of a neologism introduced solely for the rhyme.

In his subject-matter he is even more inclined to focus on his own personal concerns, or to use himself as a *persona*, than Primas: he features in every poem, with the exception of the apparently fragmentary VIII, and often depicts his poverty and grim circumstances in language at least as extreme as the earlier poet's. In I,36 he is 'dying of thirst and of starvation'; in III (as also in IV,21–2) he is coughing consumptively and close to death; in VI he is almost naked ('*nudus*', he calls himself in line 18, but he admits in the next line to possessing some vestiges of clothing, if only dreadful rags). In nearly every poem he asks for gifts of some kind, whether clothing, money, wine, or, in I,40–2, almost anything from everyone, rich or poor.

His fondness for hyperbole also inflates his praise of the Archchancellor, notably in poem VII, where no superlative is too great for him; generosity being so crucially admirable in the Archpoet's eyes he makes play here and in I,39 with the conceit that his patron is more generous than St Martin, who was a byword for that virtue because he gave half a cloak to a beggar (the fact that it was the saint's own, and only, cloak being conveniently ignored by the poet).

However, there is a subtle ironist behind the rhetoric. The poverty-stricken poet grovelling before his powerful master is very much a *persona*, as Jackson emphasises in 'The Politics of a Poet', where he gives an acute analysis of how this self-representation of the Archpoet contrasts with 'the independent, superior and quite unrepentant poet who is well aware of his value to his patron'. As Jackson makes clear, the latter *persona* is in evidence in poem IX, which, far from being the simple hymn of praise to the emperor which it purports to be, constantly undermines its own rhetoric by veiled sarcasm. Although the poet begins by declaring that it is the duty of all loyal subjects to 'render tribute unto Caesar' (partly, he admits, because it is dangerous not to), his choice of biblical imagery emphasises the contrast between spiritual values and the actual behaviour of the emperor, so that in the end 'the tribute due to Caesar has been vastly exceeded by the powers which Barbarossa has abrogated to himself'. If in this poem the Archpoet was writing the eulogy to the emperor's achievements which he had declined to write in poem IV, he was doing so very much on his own terms.

Poem IV, which incorporates that refusal, goes on to describe the stressful conditions of a poet's life, the sources of his inspiration, and his need for material support. It is intimately connected with poem X, the famous 'Confession'. Indeed the two poems have six strophes in common: IV,10–15 are repeated in X,14–19. This passage is central to the Archpoet's conception of himself as being at the mercy of his own nature: he can write only with a full stomach and an adequate amount of good wine inside him; when Bacchus has taken charge, then Apollo rushes in bringing inspiration.

The whole of poem X, with its comical/repentant portrait of the typical Goliardic poet, drunken, sensual and dissolute, is a tour de force. The Archpoet is both satirising and excusing himself, and he does so in language which subtly echoes not only biblical texts but a range of classical literature. Many commentators have listed these sources or discussed them in detail; Watenphul and Krefeld are admirably thorough, as always, and more recent treatments include Jill Mann's 'Satiric Subject and Satiric Object in Goliardic literature' and Peter Dronke's 'The Archpoet and the Classics'.

Professor Dronke has also applied his skills, in 'The Art of the Archpoet', to poem I, which is equally glittering but quite different in tone. Much of it reads like a straight-forward exposition of Christian doctrines; only towards the end, after a few stanzas flattering his influential audience, does the poet move smoothly into a brief sermon on charity and then whisk aside his preacher's robes to show the beggar's costume underneath. In strophe 37 he confesses: 'I've only one vice; I like receiving. . .' The last part of the poem is an intricately woven texture of biblical echoes and allusions, leading to his final plea for cash.

The Archpoet is never at a loss for entertaining or attractive ways of leading up to his inevitable appeal. Poem VI tells a tale of how he had to abandon his medical studies in Salerno because he caught a fever; in poem V (one of my own favourites) he is carried up to heaven in a vision and has some instructive conversation with saints and angels. This is presented in a suitably reverent (or mock-reverent) tone, but with typical little touches of humour to puncture any pretentiousness: back on earth the poet is (not for the first time) 'at death's door', but he still finds it impossible to forgive the Count Palatine for causing inflation in the price of wine.

The Archpoet is admittedly a more polished performer than Hugh Primas, but both sparkle with wit, vigour and technical ingenuity. I should not like to have to choose between them. Translating them into verse, though, has sometimes been a mixed pleasure – often rewarding, always challenging, and occasionally frustrating to a degree which made me admit defeat. My aim was always to convey the sense accurately while preserving as much of the form as I could manage. The fact that English is a far less homogeneous language than Latin means that rhyme is correspondingly more difficult to achieve within the constraints of the original meaning. There have had to be compromises: long sequences of tirade rhyme were impossible, under the circumstances, and in many cases I had to settle for half-rhymes or even less satisfactory substitutes. In poem 16 of Primas I had to abandon any thought of rhyme altogether and content myself with aiming at a reasonably acceptable pattern of rhythm. But any English translation can be only secondary to the work of the poets themselves. For the pleasures of exact rhyme, combined with metrical or rhythmical perfection, readers need only turn to the Latin.

Hugh Primas and the Archpoet: some historical (and unhistorical) testimonies

For the career of Hugh Primas, we have a range of anecdotal evidence outside his poems; for that of the Archpoet, nothing beyond what can be gleaned from the poems themselves.

In a number of sources Primas is said to be 'of Orléans'; but the earliest and best-known testimony (the passage added to Richard of Poitiers's *Chronicle, c.* 1171) links him also with Paris:

> In those days [1142] there flourished in Paris an academic named Hugh – whom his colleagues nicknamed 'the Primate' – wretched of aspect, misshapen of face. He had been imbued with secular literature from his earliest years, and the renown of his name grew radiant in diverse provinces, because of his elegant wit and literary sensibility. Among his colleagues he was most eloquent and quick-witted (*promtus*) in making verses, as we can see from the ones he composed by way of declamation (*declamatorie composuit*), making all who heard them laugh aloud, about a poor cloak that a certain bishop had given him: 'From Hugh, Primate of Orléans: *Hoc indumentum   tibi quis dedit? an fuit emptum?'* [the incipit of Poem 2B].

It has recently been argued[1] that these sentences contain no independent information, but draw upon and embroider details from Primas' poems, chiefly from the opening of Poem 23. This is indeed possible – we know that such embroidering was a common procedure in southern France, in the elaboration of 'lives' (*vidas*) of twelfth-century troubadours, and of 'commentaries' (*razos*) explaining the circumstances in which they had composed particular songs. What is certain is that, whatever element of biographical truth this chronicler's note – or Primas' poems – may contain, a decade or so after the poet's death (probably *c.* 1160) the personal myth he had created in his lifetime was alive and well.

The expressions *promtus* and *declamatorie composuit* indicate, I think, that one of the gifts for which Primas had been famous was that of composing impromptu. This is borne out by the anecdotes in Francesco

---

[1] F. Cairns, 'The Addition to the "Chronica" of Richard of Poitiers', *Mittellateinisches Jahrbuch* 19 (1984) 159–61, where the Latin is cited.

Pippino's chronicle (cited by Meyer, pp. 4–5). When Pope Lucius (whose name means 'pike') refused Primas a benefice, the poet 'inveighed against him with these verses: "Lucius is the king fish and the tyrant of the waters…"'[2] And according to the same source, in the Roman Curia Primas defeated a rival claimant to the title of supreme versifier. The cardinals set a competition, to see who could make the briefest possible verse epitome of the Old and New Testaments. Where the unnamed rival poet needed four verses (which Francesco says are lost), Primas composed only two dazzling leonine hexameters, in which each word in the first verse (on the Old Testament) rhymes with the corresponding word in the second (on the New):

> Quos   anguis   tristi   virus   mulcedine   pavit,
> Hos   sanguis   Christi   mirus   dulcedine   lavit.

> Those whom the snake's poison ravaged with doomed pleasure,
> the wondrous blood of Christ has washed with gentleness.

The anti-papal and the biblical improvisations are brilliant, and are not undeservedly ascribed to the poet from Orléans.[3] Yet whether they are really his or not is perhaps less important than that they became part of his myth: they are 'in character'. Primas – the poet with misshapen face and matchless virtuosity of tongue – was perceived, we might say, as the Cyrano de Bergerac of his day.

He was also perceived as the poet who, by his eccentric humour, could strip the high and mighty of their pretensions. This aspect of his myth is stressed in Boccaccio's story about 'Primasso' (*Decameron* I, 7), which medieval Latinists have generally ignored. Here Primas, world-famous both as teacher of literature and as poet, but ragged in looks and hence – as in his poems – easily victimised, travels from Paris to see the splendour of entertainment of the great Abbot of Cluny, who was lodging nearby. The Abbot, deceived by appearances, refuses to let Primas be served dinner; and the poet, sitting out his humiliation calmly, eating one by one the three breadrolls he had brought with him for emergencies, shames the prelate, who at last learns the identity of his

---

[2] If the ascription of the verses to Primas is correct, the reference must be to Lucius II (1144–5), rather than, as Francesco claims, to Lucius III (1181–5), during whose reign the poet, if still alive, would have been about ninety years old.

[3] On other attributions of verses and songs to Hugh Primas, see especially K. Langosch, *Hymnen und Vagantenlieder* (Basel-Stuttgart 1954), pp. 292–4. To me the majestic sequence in honour of the Cross, *Laudes crucis attollamus* (text and tr. in F. Brittain, *The Penguin Book of Latin Verse*, pp. 185–9), and the macaronic satire against greed, *In nova fert animus* (text in *Zeitschrift für deutsches Altertum* 49 (1908) 181–5), are among the most notable and most plausible ascriptions.

distinguished but poorly dressed visitor, and in remorse sends him back to Paris on a palfrey, with gifts of money and noble robes. Boccaccio's story too may have been elaborated from Primas' poetry (cf. especially the close of Poem 16); yet it is clear that, in Italy *c.* 1350, the myth of Primas remained intact and the message of his verses potent.

The allusions in Poem 16 to elections of bishops in Sens and Beauvais allow us to date this piece to 1144/5 (cf. Meyer, p. 24); since Primas here calls himself 'more than fifty years old', he will have been born in the early 1090s. The Archpoet, whose datable poems (II, IV, V, VII, IX, X) all fall within the years 1162–4, will probably have been thirty to forty years younger. (In his *Confessio*, X 7, he counts himself among the *iuvenes*: while technically a *iuvenis* can be any age between twenty-one and fifty, it would seem plausible to imagine the Archpoet as thirty or thirty-five at the time of this composition, and to set his birth not too far from 1130.) Strangely, the Franciscan chronicler Salimbene (d. 1288) confuses and conflates Primas and the Archpoet, and believes that his composite poet flourished in 1233. But in the autograph manuscript of his chronicle, while he makes Primas into a 'canon of Cologne' and ascribes to him, among other verses, the Archpoet's *Confessio* (X), Salimbene also corrected himself, adding later, in his own hand, 'Note that Primas was an Orléanais' (*Nota quod Primas Aurelianensis fuit* – cf. Meyer, p. 3). Presumably the Archpoet's way of addressing his patron as 'Archbishop-elect of Cologne' (X 24) inspired Salimbene's guess that the poet had held some office in that city – yet this guess is as wild as his date 1233 and his failure to distinguish the younger poet from the older. Clearly he took 'Primas' and 'Archipoeta' to be synonyms, since each of the two poets had affirmed himself supreme in his calling.

The careers of both were secular. There is no evidence that either of them ever became a priest, though in the course of their Liberal Arts studies (specialising in *grammatica* and the classical authors) they could well have taken minor orders. Hugh went on to teach literature, at Orléans, Paris and probably other northern French cathedral schools (his verses reveal familiarity with Amiens, Beauvais, Reims and Sens); the Archpoet, by contrast, after an attempt to study medicine in Salerno, frustrated by ill health (VI), became linked professionally with Barbarossa's imperial court. As his poems indicate, he was himself of knightly birth (*ortus ex militibus*, IV 8), and he travelled with the courtly retinue to northern Italy (VII, IX, X), Vienne (II), and Cologne (V). Nonetheless, a 'La Bohème' image of this poet – impoverished, consumptive, half-naked and half-starved – an image based on too naïve a reading of his begging-poetry – prevailed from the Romantic period until very recently. As I wrote in 1968, in an attempt to redress the balance:

> He was in fact a court poet, perhaps also a civil servant or minor diplomat, in the service of the Imperial Chancellor, and so almost certainly a member of the circle around Frederick Barbarossa himself. I am convinced that his leitmotif of the wayward, wretched vagabond-poet who is compelled to beg from his patron and his audience contains far less autobiography than literary craft... [It was used] for the sophisticated entertainment of that international set of diplomats and legislators, high-born scholars and prelates who surrounded the Emperor, whose *lingua franca* was Latin, and among whom the Archpoet probably, by his birth and position, moved as an equal.[4]

This revised picture has meanwhile been accepted by a number of German scholars. At the same time there have been two recent attempts in Germany to revert to at least one aspect of Salimbene's garbled account – to identify the Archpoet, after all, with a canon of Cologne. Two candidates, each called Rodulfus (neither of them a Rodolfo of Puccini's kind, but securely placed, prominent academics), have been proposed. The arguments, however, seem to me to show more fantasy than critical rigour. In the earlier essay (1990)[5], Rudolf Schieffer argues that one of the anonymous notaries in the Emperor's chancellery – known to specialists as 'Rainald H' (i.e. the eighth notary to appear in Chancellor Rainald's records) – has various unusual expressions and stylistic mannerisms. (These, it should perhaps be noted in passing, are *not* paralleled at any point in the Archpoet's extant verse.) Schieffer goes on to claim that, when we can document the travels of 'Rainald H' and the Archpoet, they were in the same places in the same periods of time. If both were in the imperial retinue, this would not, in my view, be surprising; yet closer scrutiny shows that Schieffer has established their coincidence in only one case (Poem IX) among the six Archpoet compositions that are more or less datable, and has shown it to be possible – not proven – in the case of two others (II and X). Schieffer's next move is to claim that the words *notarius noster Rodulfus*, written by 'Rainald H' in a document of April 1164, constitute a self-reference. No evidence is adduced for this assertion, nor for the further one, dependent on it, that this notary Rodulfus is identical with the Rodulfus who for decades was

---

[4] *The Medieval Lyric* (London 1968), pp. 21–2 (German editions, *Die Lyrik des Mittelalters*, Munich 1973 and 1977).
[5] 'Bleibt der Archipoeta anonym?', *Mitteilungen des Instituts für Österreichische Geschichtsforschung* 98 (1990) 59–79.

in charge of the cathedral school in Cologne. In other words, while it is *not impossible* that the Archpoet was 'Rainald H', or that 'Rainald H' was a notary called Rodulfus, or that this notary was the Rodulfus who taught in Cologne, all this remains wholly unsubstantiated. In a subsequent essay Johannes Fried[6], accepting Schieffer's tissue of speculations, has drawn from it a different conclusion. At the time of the Archpoet's *Confessio* (1162/3), Schieffer's Rodulfus had financial security in Cologne – where he was not replaced till 1166 – and hence, according to Fried, is unlikely to have addressed a begging-poem to Rainald of Dassel in those years. Fried would therefore make a younger Cologne master, a second Rodulfus, who did not die till 1201, his candidate for being the Archpoet.

Neither of these two proposed identifications seems to me plausible. It is *prima facie* improbable that the Archpoet should have lived until 1201: the later years of the reign of Barbarossa (d.1190) are richly documented, yet there is no trace of this poet or his poetry after 1164. More important, in the years that the Archpoet *is* attested, I believe he is most unlikely to have had any regular connection with Cologne. The reason for this lies in the wording of his appeal to Rainald (III 14): writing in Italy, he says:

Et transmontanos,   vir transmontane, iuva nos.

That is, help me because we are both from northern Europe, both from beyond the Alps. If the Archpoet, like the teachers called Rodulfus, had been Rainald's fellow-townsman (*concivis*), would he not have 'claimed kindred there, and had his claims allowed'? If he had come to Italy not just from northern Europe but from Cologne, one can almost imagine the kind of hexametrical plea this might have prompted him to make:

Inter concives   concivem suscipe, vives!

('Among fellow-townsmen, welcome your fellow-townsman, and you shall thrive!' – though the Archpoet's formulation, to be sure, would have sparkled more wittily.)

We simply cannot tell from where, north of the Alps, the Archpoet came. I have suggested ('The Archpoet and the Classics', p. 72) that around the mid-twelfth century he was probably a disciple of Primas at

---

6 'Der Archipoeta – ein Kölner Scholaster?', in *Ex ipsis rerum documentis. Festschrift für Harald Zimmermann*, ed. K. Herbers *et al.* (Jan Thorbecke Verlag, Sigmaringen, 1991, pp. 85–90). I am deeply grateful to Professor Fried for letting me see his essay prior to its publication.

Orléans: not only because he inherited certain poetic themes and techniques from Primas, but because Orléans had a school where – exceptionally at that time – one could read the rarest classical poets, such as Propertius and Tibullus, whom the Archpoet subtly plays upon in his verse. But Orléans was attracting scholars from all over Europe, and this particular non-Italian might have hailed from Prague as easily as from Paris. It has often been maintained that he was German, and this cannot be ruled out, though there is no evidence in its favour. Unfortunately claiming the Archpoet for Germany has tended to be linked to an insensitive, German-oriented reading of his poem to Barbarossa (IX), which even today is still often given the inept and historically baseless title 'Hymn to the Emperor' (*Kaiserhymnus*). This singular composition, however, amid its praises, repeatedly reminds us of the ambiguities of imperial power and of the disturbing questions that such power raises. As a national indicator, the poem cannot serve.

The Archpoet's poems I–VIII are preserved together in a small Göttingen manuscript, in which they were discovered by Jacob Grimm. Each bears the superscription 'Archipoeta' (though it has been trimmed away above Poem I). The fragment VIII comes at the end of a gathering. The loss of the next gathering in this manuscript, which would have given us the rest of Poem VIII and presumably further 'Archipoeta' poems, is incalculably great. He himself claimed that sometimes he 'composed a thousand verses swiftly' (IV 8), and there has been no shortage of attempts to ascribe to him poems beyond the ten that are given below[7]. Yet in my view nothing else has been found that both shows the individual qualities of his art and is worthy of that art.

PETER DRONKE

[7] Schieffer takes up two older suggestions – that the Archpoet might have composed an anonymous (and wholly conventional) sequence, *Urbs Aquensis, urbs regalis (Analecta Hymnica* 55, no. 201), for the canonisation of Charlemagne (Christmas 1165), as well as the satire *Utar contra vitia (Carmina Burana* no. 42). The second is a brilliant composition, but much closer in style to the Archpoet's contemporary, Walter of Châtillon (to whom it is indeed ascribed in the bilingual edition of the *Carmina Burana*, Zurich-Munich 1974). Fried makes a brave attempt to give the Archpoet the five additional strophes of the *Confessio* that are preserved uniquely in the *Carmina Burana* (no. 191a) – but I find it hard to see them as on the same artistic level as the 25 strophes printed as Poem x below. For other attributions, see G. Bernt, 'Archipoeta', in *Verfasser-Lexikon* I (1978) 426.

Hugh Primas

1

Hospes erat michi se plerumque professus amicum,
    voce michi prebens plurima, re modicum.
Quis fuerat taceo, si quis de nomine querat;
4   sed qualis possum dicere: rufus erat.
Hic dum me recipi summa bonitate putarem,
    intravi plenum fraude doloque larem.
Me domini fratrem consanguineumve putares;
8   sic domus et dominus excipiunt hilares.
Tunc dominus cepit vicibus me plangere crebris,
    illaqueare volens talibus illecebris:
'Dedecus est, Primas, quod sit quadrupes tibi solus.'
12   Non erat hoc pietas; fraus erat atque dolus.
Dum moror, evenit michi quadam forte dierum
    sumere plus solito forte recensque merum.
Unde piger cene post horam splendidioris
16   ebrius optabam menbra locare thoris.
Hospes at astutus obliquo lumine ridet
    nutantemque parum scire videre videt.
'Non' ait, 'est sanum dormire, sumus quia pleni.
20   Ludere tres solidos, hospes amice, veni!'
Denariis inhians paucis misereque crumene,
    'Quin etiam decios, si placet, ante tene!'
Ad mea dampna citus properans post gaudia cene
24   proieci decios: non cecidere bene.
Hospes eos iecit michi fallaces, sibi fidos:
    infelix Primas perdidit v solidos.
Vina dabant verne sapientes atque periti
28   et 'bibe', dicabant, 'ne moriare siti.'
Me potasse prius de nil constante putavi:
    nunc scio, quod dampno vina fuere gravi.
Paulatim caput incipiens dimittere pronum,
32   paulatim cepit perdere bursa sonum.
Queque prius grandi residebat turgida culo,
    evacuata iacens ore tacet patulo.
Que fuit in cena fecunda, loquax, bene plena,
36   nec vox nec sonitus mansit ei penitus.
Infelix Decius talem confundat amicum,
38   qui sic nostra tulit, quod nichil est reliquum.

2

1

My host was my good friend, or so he would profess:
lavish with words, he gave me in actual fact much less.
I shan't reveal his name, should anyone enquire;
but I can say what he was like: he had red hair.   4
Thinking I'd met with a most generous reception,
I stepped into a den of trickery and deception.
You'd think I was the master's brother or close kin,
so joyfully did house and master take me in.   8
But then the man began a list of lamentations,
and tried to lure me into trouble through deceptions:
'Primas, you've only got one horse: that isn't right.'
This wasn't kindliness, but treachery and deceit.   12
While I was there, it happened that I consumed one day
some rather strong new wine, and more than was my way.
After the over-sumptuous meal I longed to sink
wearily into bed; I'd had too much to drink.   16
My cunning host, amused, gave me a sidelong look
and saw me nodding, scarcely able to keep awake.
'To sleep when we're so full', he told me, 'isn't wise.
Come on, my guest and friend, let's play three-guinea dice.'   20
Greedily viewing my few coins and meagre purse
he added 'If it suits you, why don't you throw first?'
So, rushing headlong to my ruin on the swell
of the feast, I threw the dice: they didn't fall out well.   24
The dice were false to me, but loyal to my host
when his throw came; 5 guineas were what poor Primas lost.
The servants plied me still with wine: 'You mustn't die
of thirst, so please drink up!' they said, well-taught and sly.   28
I fancied, at the time, free wine had come my way;
but now I know the heavy price I had to pay.
Gradually my purse's head began to sink,
and gradually the purse began to lose its clink.   32
The thing that once, broad-buttocked, had sat there, swollen stout,
was lying open-mouthed and silent, emptied out.
What had been talkative, well-stocked and nicely round
at dinner-time, was now without a voice or sound.   36
May evil-dealing Decius curse that kind of friend
who took my all, and left me with nothing in the end.   38

2

A

Pontificum spuma,   fex cleri, sordida struma,
qui dedit in bruma   michi mantellum sine pluma!

B

'Hoc indumentum   tibi quis dedit? an fuit emptum?
4 estne tuum?' 'Nostrum;   sed qui dedit abstulit ostrum.'
'Quis dedit hoc munus?'   'Presul michi prebuit unus.'
'Qui dedit hoc munus   dedit hoc in munere funus.
Quid valet in bruma   clamis absque pilo, sine pluma?
8 cernis adesse nives: moriere gelu neque vives.'

C

'Pauper mantelle,   macer, absque pilo, sine pelle,
si potes, expelle   boream rabiemque procelle!
sis michi pro scuto,   ne frigore pungar acuto!
12 per te posse puto   ventis obsistere tuto.'
Tunc ita mantellus: 'Michi nec pilus est neque vellus.
sum levis absque pilo,   tenui sine tegmine filo.
te mordax aquilo   per me feriet quasi pilo.
16 si notus iratus   patulos perflabit hiatus,
stringet utrumque latus   per mille foramina flatus.'
'Frigus adesse vides.'   'Video, quia frigore strides:
sed michi nulla fides,   nisi pelliculas clamidi des.
20 Scis, quid ages, Primas?   eme pelles, obstrue rimas!
tunc bene depellam,   iuncta michi pelle, procellam.
Conpatior certe,   moveor pietate super te
23 et facerem iussum,   sed Jacob, non Esau sum.'

3

Orpheus Euridice   sociatur, amicus amice,
matre canente dea,   dum rite colunt hymenea.
In luctum festa   vertit lux tercia mesta.
4 Pressus enim planta   spatiantis gaudia tanta
serpens dissolvit,   qui languidus ora resolvit,

2

A

The scum of the priesthood, clerical dregs, a disgusting sore –
the man who, in winter, gave me an unlined cloak to wear!

B

'That cloak you're wearing – who gave it to you? Or did you buy it?
It's yours, is it?' 'Yes, but the donor cut the trimmings off it.'   4
'Who gave you that present?' 'It was a bishop who gave it.'
'The man who gave the present gave you a death sentence with it.
What's the use, in winter, of a cloak with no fur or feather?
Look, it's going to snow; you'll freeze to death in this weather.'   8

C

'Poor thin cloak, without a lining of fur or leather,
try, if you can, to keep out the north wind and the wild weather.
Don't let me freeze in the cold; shield me, keep me warm!
With your help I think I can safely survive a storm.'   12
Then the cloak replied: 'I have neither fur nor skin.
I'm light and without a lining; my fabric is bare and thin.
Through me the sharp north wind will hit you like a javelin.
If the angry southerly should blow through my open places   16
its gusts will chill both sides of you through a thousand gaping spaces.'
'You can see it's winter.' 'I can see, because it's making you shiver.
But don't rely on me, unless you line your cloak with leather.
You know what to do, Primas? Buy skins and fill in the cracks!   20
Then, leather-lined, I'll efficiently ward off the storm's attacks.
I'm truly sympathetic, and properly conscious of your claim
to my services; but a Jacob, not an Esau, is what I am.'   23

3

Eurydice is joined   to Orpheus, her loving friend;
the muse his mother's singing   accompanies their formal wedding.
But then on the third morning   their celebration turns to
        mourning.

ledens ledentem   dum figeret in pede dentem.
Lesa iacet feno   pede vipera, nupta veneno.
8 Percipit et pallet.   Puto, quod sua funera mallet.
Nec minus exanguis   fit homo quam nupta vel anguis.
Sed quid agat? Fleret?   Sed quid sibi flere valeret?
Non est flere viri.   Videt et iubet hanc sepuliri,
12 et residet iuxta   suspirans menbra venusta.
Menbra tegit petra,   sed habent animam loca tetra.
Nil lacrimas vidit   prodesse, sed in fide fidit.
Rem meditans grandem   tacito sub pectore tandem:
16 'Est', ait, 'in cordis   celestibus altus honor dis.
Non facit esse parum   sua patrem dis lyra carum.
Sic te posse puto   leniri carmine, Pluto.
Mulcebo Parcas,   ut voce deos deus Archas.'
20 Ergo fides aptat,   movet, ordinat atque retractat
per voces octo   digitis et pollice docto,
confisusque lyre   post umbram destinat ire.
Ut stetit ad fluctus,   quos dicit Grecia luctus,
24 dans obolum naute   subit et sedet, ast ita caute,
ne titubare gravis   valeat pre pondere navis.
Iamque lyra sumpta   devectus trans Acerunta
constitit ante fores,   regem videt atque priores.
28 Rex ait in causis   hominum de tristibus ausis,
dicere ne cesset,   quid querat sive quis esset.
Ammonitus tuto   sic inchoat ore soluto,
verba sequente sono,   cum plebe tacente patrono:
32 'Te primum, Pluto,   regem dominumque saluto.
Extremo fratrum   tibi cessit sorte baratrum;
cesserit extrema   tibi sorte licet diadema,
sis licet extremus: tua nos plus iura timemus.
36 Quotquot enim vivi   sumus, huc erimus recidivi
ocius aut sero,   sub iudicis ore severo
iuste laturi   sontes mala premia puri.
Iustis et reprobis   erit omnibus hec via nobis.
40 Huc venisse virum   dicet tua curia mirum.
Cur veniam vivus,   latet hos, tu scis quia divus.
Separat a superis   me dulcis amor mulieris,
que non natura   neque morbo, sed nece dura,
44 nec nece matura,   sed vi venit in tua iura.
Prosit, quod canto,   quod regi servio tanto;

A snake, on which the bride   stepped as she walked along, has   4
    made
an end of all their joys   by opening its dying jaws
and wounding with its fang   the foot of her who caused its pang.
They lie there, snake and woman,   one crushed, the other dead of
    poison.
Orpheus sees, aghast: he'd have laid down his own life first.   8
He has so pale a look   he seems as dead as bride and snake.
But what can he do? Weep?   But how can weeping be a help?
Men don't cry. So he's ordered   his dear one's body to be buried
and, staying near the place,   sighs for her beauty and her grace.   12
Her body's in the tomb;   her soul is in the realms of gloom.
Since weeping is a waste   of time, his lyre is what he'll trust.
At last a daring plot   emerges from his silent thought:
he says 'High honour's given   to music by the gods in heaven.   16
When the immortals hear   my father's lyre they hold him dear.
So I believe that you, too,   can be appeased by singing, Pluto.
As divine Mercury's tongue   charms gods, I'll charm the Fates by
    song.'
So he proceeds to tune   his instrument: adjusts the tone,   20
runs through the octave, strums   the strings with fingers and
    skilled thumb;
trusting his lyre to aid   his quest, he goes after her shade.
When he's beside the river   the Greeks call 'Sorrow', he hands over
the boatman's penny fare   and steps on board, but sits with care   24
so that the loaded boat   won't tilt and wobble with his weight.
Then on the further shore   of Acheron, holding his lyre,
he stops before the gate   and sees the king there with his court.
The king, who's busy hearing   cases concerned with human   28
    daring,
tells him to say at once   who he may be and what he wants.
Orpheus, at his urging,   begins to speak out freely, matching
his music to the words,   while silence falls on crowd and lord:
'First of all, great Pluto,   king and master, I salute you.   32
Chance gave you for your portion,   as the last brother, this deep
    region;
but though your royal crown   was the last to be assigned –
Yes, though you are the last,   yours are the judgements we fear
    most.
All of us now alive   sooner or later must arrive   36
here; the reward we've earned   will be delivered by the stern

non sine mercede   tanta dimittar ab ede.
Nec michi magna peto: redeat mea nupta, iubeto!
48 Sit cythare merces,   quam sub loca dura coherces!
Nec sum importunus   neque perpetuum peto munus:
parvam quero moram   neque perpetuo sed ad horam.
Hac veniam comite   celeris post gaudia vite;
52 Mors, que nos solvet,   caput huc utrumque resolvet.'

4

Flare iube lentos   et lenes, Eole, ventos:
carcere contentos   coibe celeres, violentos!
Prodeat e claustro   comitante Favonius Austro:
4 istos flare iube   sine nimbis et sine nube!
Cesset flare parum   gelidus turbator aquarum,
ne voret Imarum   mare triste, vorax et avarum!
Sic ferat Imarum,   quod ei mare non sit amarum;
8 pondus tam carum   Zephirus ferat et mare clarum!

Non via terrarum,   sed me via terret aquarum.
'Cur mare te terret?'   Quia me mare non bene ferret;
cumque fretum verret,   vereor, ne navis oberret.
12 More volantis avis   volat alta per equora navis
planiciemque salis   velut ales transvolat alis.
Me ratis alata,   me terret et unda salata.
Si ruat in cautem,   ratis est factura 'Tu autem',
16 et rate confracta   de me sunt omnia facta.

voice of the judge: punishment   for the guilty, blessings for the
    innocent.
Whether we're good or bad   we're all condemned to tread this
    road.
That I've come here alive   your courtiers scarcely will believe: 40
they can't guess why a man   might come (you know, being
    divine).
I left the world above   for my dear wife's sake, out of love;
she died unnaturally,   not of disease, but cruelly;
her death was premature;   by force she came into your power.   44
Reward the song I sing,   my service to so great a king;
let me not leave your grand   residence with empty hands.
It isn't much I seek: command that my wife may go back!
Let my musician's fee   be her, your prisoner: set her free!   48
It's quite a modest favour   I ask; it needn't last for ever:
a short reprieve will do –   not for eternity, just for now.
I'll come here with my wife   after a swift but joyful life;
when we're undone by death   you'll be repaid: you'll have us   52
    both.'

4

Aeolus, order slow   and very gentle winds to blow;
the violent, swift ones tell   to stay contented in their cell.
Release from prison just   two of your winds, the South and West;
and let them bring no cloud   or showers: these are not allowed!   4
Forbid the North, the chill   wave-roughener, to blow at all,
lest Imarus should be   gulped by the grim, devouring sea.
May he enjoy a calm   sea, such as will not do him harm.
Let Zephyr guide the dear   cargo, and let the sea be clear.   8

I'm not afraid on land   but sea-borne travel I can't stand.
'Why do you fear the sea?'   Well, it may not be kind to me.
I fear the ship may stray   off course when sweeping over the sea.
With a birdlike motion   the ship flies over the deep ocean   12
and like a thing sustained   by wings it skims the salty plain.
I fear both the winged boat   and the salt waves that make it float.
If it should hit a reef   all I possess will come to grief;
a shipwreck spells the end   for me: 'Tu autem' and Amen.   16

5

Ulceribus plenus   victum petit eger, egenus:
dives non audit,   victum negat, hostia claudit;
dum sanies manat,   lingens canis ulcera sanat.
4 Angelus evexit,   quem nec vetus instita texit:
purpura quem texit,   stridet, cum spiritus exit.
Perpetuo digne   miser est et pauper in igne,
pauperis et miseri   qui non voluit misereri.
8 Vidit nec novit   nec pavit eum neque fovit:
nunc videt et noscit   et aquas a paupere poscit.
Gaudet, qui flevit: cruciatur, qui requievit,
qui miserum sprevit,   quem splendida cena replevit.
12 Esurit in pena,   quem pavit splendida cena;
vina bibens quondam   sitit et videt et petit undam
14 iudicioque dei   datur ignibus: hic requiei.

6

Idibus his Mai   miser exemplo Menelai
flebam nec noram   quis sustulerat michi Floram.
Tempus erat florum,   cum flos meus, optimus horum,
4 liquit Flora thorum,   fons fletus, causa dolorum.
Nam dum, Flora, fugis,   remanet dolor iraque iugis,
et dolor et cure,   nisi veneris, haut abiture.
Cur non te promis,   dulcis comes et bene comis,
8 ut redeunte pari   comites pellantur amari?
Terris atque fretis   vagor, expers luce quietis
per noctem somni,   capto captivior omni.
Omni captivo   vel paupere vel fugitivo
12 pauperior vivo.   Madet et iugi gena rivo
nec fiet sicca,   manus hanc nisi tergat amica.
Si remeare velis,   tunc liber, tunc ero felix;
maior ero vates   quam Cyrus sive Phraates,
16 vincam primates   et regum prosperitates.
Quod si forte lates,   aliquos ingressa penates,
exi, rumpe moram;   mora sit brevis hic et ad horam.
Alter fortassis   precio te transtulit assis,
20 vilis et extremus   neque noscens, unde dolemus.

5

A sick man, full of sores,   begged food because he was so poor;
the rich man wouldn't hear,   denied him food and shut the door.
A dog was licking clean   the ulcers out of which pus ran.
An angel carried off   the man without a rag of stuff;   4
the man in purple cloth   was screaming when his soul went forth.
Wretched and poor, he burned   in endless fire: a fate he earned
because he had no pity   for wretchedness and poverty.
He saw, and understood   nothing; he gave no alms or food;   8
but now sees, understands,   asks water from the beggar's hands.
The man who wept's contented;   the comfortable one's tormented:
the man who scorned the beggar,   having enjoyed a splendid
    dinner,
is tortured now with hunger   and fed with splendid food no longer. 12
He who drank wine in the past   now sees and begs water for his
    thirst:
for under God's decrees   he burns; the beggar lies at ease.

6

It was the Ides of May;   I wept, distressed in the same way
as Menelaus; for a   rival had lured away my Flora.
It was the flower season   when she, my flower, the finest blossom,
left where we'd been sleeping   and caused my sorrow and my   4
    weeping.
My Flora, since you've gone   the pain and anger linger on;
unless you come to me   the pain and grief won't let me be.
Why don't you show your face,   my sweet companion, full of
    grace,
so that when you've returned   that bitter company is banned?   8
On land and sea I roam;   my days are all devoid of calm,
my nights of sleep; I feel   less free than if I were in jail.
The life I lead is poorer   than that of any prisoner,
pauper or runaway.   My cheeks are wet with tears all day   12
and won't be dry again   unless your sweet hand wipes them clean.
If you'll return to me   then I'll be happy, I'll be free;
then I'll achieve great things: your poet will surpass those kings,
Cyrus and Phraates, both   in worldly status and in wealth.   16
But if you've gone to ground   in someone's house, and can't be
    found,

Ut solet absque mare   turtur gemebunda volare,
que semel orba pari   nec amat neque curat amari:
sic vagor et revolo,   recubans miser in lare solo,
24 qui mutare dolo   latus assuetum michi nolo,
turturis in morem   cui dat natura pudorem,
quod, simul uxorem   tulerit mors seva priorem,
non sit iocundum   thalamum temptare secundum.
28 Sed tu mendosa   rides me flente dolosa,
sola nec accumbis,   levibus par facta columbis,
quis calor in lumbis   mutare facit thalamum bis.

7

Quid luges, lirice,   quid meres pro meretrice?
Respira, retice   neque te dolor urat amice!
Scimus – et est aliquid –   quia te tua Flora reliquit.
4 Sed tu ne cures,   possunt tibi dicere plures,
qui simili more,   simili periere dolore.
Teque dolor scorti   dabit afflictum cito morti,
ni dure sorti   respondes pectore forti.
8 Quod mala sors prebet,   sapiens contempnere debet;
res quociens mestas   non est mutare potestas,
mesta ferendo bene   reddit paciencia lene.
Sed quin perferimus,   quod permutare nequimus!
12 Consolare lyra   luctum, quem parturit ira!
Paulum respira,   quia destino dicere mira!
Ergo quiesce parum!   Nec erit grave nec amarum,
si nunc ignarum   mores doceamus earum.
16 Lenonem lena   non diligit absque crumena.
Lance cibo plena,   vinum fundente lagena,
plus gaudet cena   quam dulce sonante Camena.
Cum nidor naso   veniet, gaudebit omaso
20 aut aliquid sorde   plus quam dulcedine corde.
Cum vestis danda   vel erit bona cena paranda,
tunc quidvis manda,   tunc semper erit tibi blanda.
Sed cum dona feret,   que nunc tibi blanda coheret,

---

[2] *amice* = *amicae* (fem. genitive sing. rather than masc. vocative) – or so I take it.

come out: don't hesitate   but hurry – please don't make me wait.
I've no doubt you were willing   to go, for something like a shilling,
to that low swine, that other   who can't imagine why I suffer.   20
Just as the turtle-dove   can neither give nor welcome love
after it's lost its mate,   but flies around, disconsolate,
so I fly to and fro,   then sleep alone and full of woe.
I'd think it a betrayal   to change my partner: I'm the loyal   24
turtle-dove, to whom   nature has given a sense of shame,
so that, when cruel fate   has snatched away its former mate,
to have a second try   at marriage offers it no joy.
But you, you faithless lying   deceiver, laughing when I'm crying,   28
you won't lie down alone;   you're like that other dove, the one
whom sexual heat impels   to change its mate for someone else.

7

What are you grieving for,   poet? Why cry over a whore?
Control yourself and stop   before this heartbreak burns you up.
I know that you're bereft   (why not?) because your Flora's left.
But don't be too upset: that's the advice you'd surely get   4
from lots who've pined away   grief-stricken in a similar way.
Your pangs over this tart,   unless you face with a stout heart
what cruel fate can do,   will surely be the death of you.
A man ought to despise   the blows fate deals him, if he's wise;   8
Whenever there's no power   to change things, sad although they
        are,
if we bear them well,   patience can soften the ordeal.
So why not just endure   what after all we'll never cure?
Use poetry to soothe   the sorrow anger has brought forth!   12
Stop crying for a spell: I've an amazing tale to tell.
So, silence for a moment!   It won't be so grim or unpleasant
if I enlighten you   about just what these women do.
A lover with no wallet   means nothing to a prostitute.   16
She takes more pleasure in a   dish piled lavishly with dinner
and a carafe of wine   than poetry, however fine.
The smell that greets her nostrils   from tripe or any filthy offal
will lift her spirits higher   than lovely music on the lyre.   20
Whenever there's some clothing   or a good meal in the offing,
then she'll do anything   you tell her, constantly obliging.
But once she's got the presents,   she who is now all compliance
will let you down, and chase   some other man to devour and fleece. 24

24 quem voret et laceret   pociorem perfida queret.
   Quo semel invento   te munere linquet adempto,
   cedet contempto   te paupere teque redempto.
   Que predam nacta,   cum res fuerit tua fracta,
28 nec bona transacta   tua nec recolet bene facta.
   Tu risus plebis   mecho ridente dolebis,
   risus eris ville,   meretrix ridebit et ille.
   Nescit enim miseris   misereri mens mulieris
32 mobilibus pueris   ventoque simillima veris.
   Quam, quia nil dederis,   modici sonus auferet eris;
   promittas rursus: velox erit inde recursus.
   Si tibi bursa sonet,   que spes modicam sibi donet,
36 bursa redire monet: revolabit eumque ponet.
   Nec nisi mendicum   mendax dimittit amicum.
   Bursa vocat mecham,   veluti vocat ad cirotecam
   crus avis excisum   vel visa caruncula nisum.
40 Sumpto quadrante   tunc iurabit tibi sancte:
   'Non dimittam te,   nisi me dimiseris ante'.
   Cum dederis ummum,   iurabit te fore summum,
   tunc finget lacrimas   partesque dabit tibi primas;
44 'alter plura licet   michi det, te plus amo' dicet,
   munus ut extricet   et totum prodiga siccet.
   Nam sua custodit,   te nescia parcere rodit,
   tardantemque fodit;   nisi des cito, quod volet, odit.
   Cumque miser tua das,   non querit, dum sibi tradas,
49 unde hoc corradas   vel egens quo denique vadas.

8

Jussa lupanari   meretrix exire, parari
provida vult ante,   quamvis te sepe vocante.
Conponit vultum,   meliorem dat sibi cultum,
4 illinit unguento   faciem, prodit pede lento.
Cum venit ingressa,   residet spirans quasi fessa
seque verecunde   venisse refert aliunde,
quamquam venit heri,   simulans timuisse videri.
8 Cuius in adventum   famulorum turba frequentum

She'll leave you, having taken   your assets, once she's found the
    new one:
she'll go away and scoff –   you're a poor man, you've been let off.
She doesn't give a hoot,   now that you're ruined and the loot's
hers, for your kindly deeds   and your attention to her needs.   28
You'll be a laughing-stock   for everyone in town to mock,
and while you're grieving   she and her lover will be laughing.
The female mind's unable   to pity anyone in trouble:
like lively boys at play   or the spring wind it flits away.   32
Because you've nothing for her   the slightest chink of cash will lure
    her;
you promise her some more: she'll come back running to your door.
If your jingling wallet   gives her the slightest hope of profit
it calls her back; she'll run   to you, and dump the other man.   36
But if he's not a beggar   the cheat will never jilt a lover.
A wallet calls a whore   just as a leg of chicken or
a scrap of meat calls back   to its master's glove a sparrowhawk.
She'll accept your money   then swear to you devotedly   40
'I shan't sent you away   unless you've first rejected me.'
When you give her a coin   she'll swear that you're her favourite
    man;
then fake some tears, to prove   you're the prime object of her love.
'Even if someone else   gives more, I love you more' she says,   44
to extract her presents   and drain you dry of all your substance.
She guards her property   and wears you down remorselessly;
and if you're slow she baits you: give what she wants *now*, or she
    hates you.
Miserably you give her   what's yours; and as you hand it over
she won't ask how you scraped   it up, or where you'll turn when   49
    bankrupt.

8

You've sent out for a whore   but she won't leave the brothel before
she's ready, never mind   how many messages you send.
She does her face and hair,   finds something prettier to wear,
rubs cream into her face,   and then sets forth with leisured pace.   4
As soon as she's arrived   she sits down panting as if tired:
she's come from somewhere else,   she says; though she came to
    your house
yesterday, she'll feign   a bashful fear of being seen.

extendit leta   cortinas atque tapeta.
Flagrat tota rosis   et m** preciosis
vestibus instrata   domus, ut sit ei mage grata.
12 Omnia magnifice   disponis pro meretrice;
maiori cura   cocus aptat fercula plura.
Que quasi morosa,   quasi comis, deliciosa
singula percurrit,   degustat, pauce ligurrit.
16 Servit tota domus.   Cum vina dat optima promus,
sorbillat paullum,   vix adprecians ea naulum.
Tecum nocte cubat   quasi virgo, que modo nubat;
clamat dum scandis,   quia res nimis ist tibi grandis;
20 anxia cum lite   iurat non posse pati te;
cumque gemens plorat,   aditum stringendo minorat:
qui si sit patulus,   vix inpleat hunc bene mulus.
Cras ubi dimittis,   obnubit timpora vittis,
24 ne quis noscat eam,   dum transvolat illa plateam.
Cum domus exilis   habet hanc, casa sordida, vilis,
tunc sibi de rivo   potum petit. In lare privo
inplent lactuce   festiva fercula luce
28 aut olus aut fungi.   Bene si quando volet ungi,
tunc emit exta bovis   sacianda cadavere quovis
vel capre vel ovis   pecudumve pedes tribus ovis;
vel panis duri   calefacto frustula iuri
32 frangens infercit,   alia cui nocte pepercit.
Vilia tunc villa,   que fece fluunt, emit illa;
fraude bacetigeri   ne quid valeat retineri,
in virga numerum   designat uterque dierum;
36 venditor et villi   metretas conputat illi
pro quadrante decem   prebens ad prandia fecem.
Tunc si scurra pedes   pede nudo pulsat ad edes,
mimus sive calo   vel suetus ludere talo,
40 pene rigente malo   celer hostia frangere palo
leno discinctus: cicius te mittitur intus.
Plus habet inde pedes   quam Peleus aut Diomedes
nobiliorve Pelops: ita currit ad hostia velox.
44 Ad vocem lixe   properat metuens ea rixe,
turpis et inconpta   post scurram currere prompta.

---

10 R has *et menta* (or *merta*) *preciosis*; something seems to have been omitted or wrongly
transcribed. Meyer prints *et m***, but suggests that a word such as *unguentis* has fallen out.
McDonough offers *unguentis* or *muneribus*; I prefer the latter.

Welcoming her advent   a happy crowd of willing servants   8
hangs curtains all around   and spreads a carpet on the ground.
Your house is all aglow   with roses and an expensive show
of gifts, and decked with hangings,   to make sure it's to her liking.
You offer splendid treats   to impress this woman of the streets;   12
the cook strains his resources   to serve a meal of many courses.
She scans the gourmet food   in a half-sweet, half-sullen mood,
permits herself a taste,   and lets most of it go to waste.
The whole house gives her homage.   The butler brings her his best   16
      vintage;
she plays at sipping it –   ignores the cost of shipping it.
At night she lies beside   you like a new and virgin bride;
you mount her, and she cries   over your thing's excessive size,
nervously struggles, swears   it's really more than she can bear;   20
and, as she groans and begs,   contracts the space between her legs –
which, if she spread it wide,   could take at least a mule inside.
When she's sent home next day   she veils her head, and goes
      away
across the street disguised   so that she won't be recognised.   24
However, when she's back   in her own house – a dirty shack –
what she drinks is water   out of a stream. In her own quarters
the food she gets to eat is,   on festive days, a plate of lettuce
or mushrooms or some kale.   To make an extra special meal   28
(any old meat will do)   she buys the innards of a cow
or of a goat or sheep,   or threepence-worth of ox's feet;
or else she takes a bit   of hard stale bread, and crushes it
into leftover soup   saved from last night, which she's warmed up.   32
Then she buys wine: cheap rubbish   full of dregs and floating
      garbage;
so that the wine-vendor   won't be able to defraud her
they both together nick   the date-notch on the tally-stick;
and the merchant reckons   her wine-jars up for her: one quadrans   36
will buy her from his kegs   ten meals' accompaniment of dregs.
Then if some common jester,   barefoot, knocks at the door for her –
a scullion, a busker,   or perhaps a hardened gambler –
armed with a stiff truncheon,   almost about to break her door in,   40
this scruffy Romeo   is let inside sooner than you.
A man on foot means more   than Peleus, Diomedes, or
great Pelops to the whore: she runs so quickly to the door.
She hurries when she hears   the oaf's voice (brawling's what she   44
      fears):

Quelibet inmunda   loca poscat, non pudibunda,
spe levis argenti   stabulo caput abdet olenti.
48 Quolibet inpelli   levis ibit amore lucelli.
Sicut apis melli   semel heret dura revelli,
sic volat ad munus   meretrix, quod scurra dat unus;
51 quo semel accepto   cuivis se vendet inepto.

9

Urbs erat illustris,   quam belli clade bilustris
nunc facit exustrix   fecundam flamma ligustris.
Urbs fecunda ducum,   caput inclinata caducum,
4 nunc fecunda nucum   stupet ex se surgere lucum.
Crescit flava seges,   dictabat rex ubi leges;
6 fedant tecta greges,   ubi nutriit Hecuba reges.
Urbs habitata viris   et odoribus inclita Syris
8 nunc domus est tigris,   serpentibus hospita diris.
Urbem reginam,   mundi decus ante ruinam,
10 terrarum dominam: videas humilem, resupinam.
Cerva facit saltus,   ubi nobilior fuit altus
12 et ludis aptus   Ganimedes a Jove raptus.
Urbs bene sublimis,   ducibus predives opimis
14 unaque de primis: modo fit minor et comes imis.
Si muros veteres,   si templa domosque videres,
16 quam tenere fleres   mala, que malus intulit heres.
Terra referta bonis,   fulgens opibus Salomonis
18 et regum donis: nunc est spelunca leonis.
Heu, quid agunt bella!   preciosa iacent capitella
20 et Jovis in cella   cubat hinc ovis, inde capella.
Urbis nunc misere   dolor est tot dampna videre,
22 que modo tota fere   gemmis radiabat et ere.
Certabat stellis: topazius in capitellis
24 et decus anellis,   medicina smaraudus ocellis.
Sardus et onichili   sordent in pulvere vili,

The text appears with significant variations in R and B. On the whole I follow Meyer,
preserving his order for lines 5–16, as in B (they are differently arranged in R); but I omit
three later couplets found in B but not in R.

grubby and untidy,   at his whim she's ever-ready.
Whatever filthy game   he asks of her she has no shame:
hoping for a small coin   she'll let him into her smelly den.
There's nowhere she won't turn   for the pittance she's so keen to   48
   earn.
As a bee sticks to honey   so does the prostitute to money:
she can't be torn away,   when once she's flown to her clown's
   pay.
She's willing to be laid   by any fool once she's been paid.   51

9

This was a glorious city, but a terrible ten years' war
has made it a fertile shrubbery, with the aid of devouring fire.
Once fertile in princes, the city lowered its death-doomed head;
now it's amazed to have grown a thicket fertile in nuts instead.   4
Golden corn grows up where Priam once pronounced his laws,
and where Hecuba suckled princes sheep defile the floors.   6
A city where men lived, a place famous for Syrian perfume,
harbours tigers now and gives venomous snakes a home.   8
Until its fall a queen, the finest city the world could show,
it ruled the earth; but now you may see it ruined and brought low.   10
Deer leap in the place where Ganymede grew up, whom Jove
snatched away – that noble youth, apt for the sports of love.   12
A city in the first rank, pre-eminent, richly blessed
with noble lords, is now reduced and joins the lowest.   14
If you could see the ancient walls, the temples and houses here,
how you would weep at the harm brought on by a harmful heir.   16
A country stuffed with goods, gleaming with wealth like Solomon's
and with the gifts of kings, has now become a den for lions.   18
This is what war does, alas: the expensive columns fall,
a sheep or a goat uses Jove's sanctum for its stall.   20
To see the damage done to this pathetic town is cruel,
when not so long ago it gleamed with shining bronze and jewels.   22
It rivalled the stars; the pillars were set with chrysolite
and emerald, which adorns rings and benefits the eyesight.   24
Sard and onyx are lying, filthy, in the dusty soil;

26 quos tulit a Nili   victoria fontibus Ili.
   Gloria matronis   et regum digna coronis
   inclita Sardonis   ictu percussa ligonis
29 occurrit pronis   vel arantibus arva colonis.
   Que modo contempta,   sed magno regibus empta,
31 venditur inventa   pro nummo sive placenta.
   Mercatorque bonus   vendit pro pane colonus
33 nobilis auris onus,   quod repperit in scrobe pronus.
   Urbs bene fecunda,   nulli sub sole secunda,
35 quod fuit immunda,   luit et patitur gemebunda.
   Quolibet in scelere   sperans sibi cuncta licere
37 sorduit in venere: sed dis ea displicuere.
   Quod Paridi fede   nubebat filia Lede
   et steriles tede   nubente Jovi Ganimede:
40 cum propria sede   luit hoc datus incola prede.
   Nostris fracta dolis   inmense fabrica molis
42 scinditur agricolis,   opus ammirabile Solis.
   Infensus divis   periit cum principe civis,
44 et cum captivis   rex captus servit Achivis.
   Urbis preclare   rex ipse volens latitare
46 fataque vitare   cum prole coheserat are;
   credebant miseri   superos debere timeri:
   ira ducis pueri   non curat sacra vereri;
49 sic nec eos superi   potuere nec ara tueri.
   Talia cum memorem,   nequeo cohibere dolorem,
51 quin de te plorem,   cum de te, Troia, perorem.
   Sed iam menbra thoris   dare nos monet hora soporis.

26   *quos*: both MSS have *quas*, which Meyer and McDonough print without comment.

10

Post rabiem rixe   redeunte bilustris Ulixe
rupibus infixe   tenuere rates vada; vix se
expedit invictus   fortune fortis ad ictus
4 et preter superos   nulli superabilis heros,
dampnis afflictus   odio superum neque victus.
Afflictus dampnis   neque victus pluribus annis
viderat Ethiopes   Arabas avidosque Ciclopes.

Meyer's text, which I follow, is based on B; R omits the first 8 lines, the final 16, and lines
63–65. In certain other details Meyer has followed R.

the victory of King Ilus brought them from the source of the Nile.   26
The noble sardonyx, fit to grace fine ladies or the brow
of royalty in a crown, is dug up by farmers now:
they hit it with a hoe, or find it as they stoop to the plough.   29
An object for which kings paid well is now a worthless trinket;
the finder holds it cheap: a penny or a cake will buy it.   31
A farmer sells for bread something he spotted in a ditch –
it was a prince's earring – and thinks the bargain's made him rich.   33
No city under the sun could match this, in its fertile prime;
it groans in anguish now, trying to expiate its crime.   35
It hoped to be allowed licence for any kind of lechery,
wallowing in its lust; but all that made the gods angry.   37
Paris's so-called marriage with Leda's daughter – a disgrace –
and the barren coupling when Jove took Ganymede as spouse:
for these Troy and its people lost their freedom and paid the price.   40
It was our tricks that brought this huge fortress to destruction;
farmers plough the site of Apollo's marvellous construction.   42
State and leader alike perished because the gods were grieved;
captured by the Greeks, both prince and people were enslaved.   44
The Trojan king himself, to avoid his fate, wanted to hide;
he clung for sanctuary to the altar, his children by his side;   46
the poor things thought the gods would inspire fear, as is their right;
but the young general was too angry to venerate
holy things; neither gods nor altar could shield them from their fate.   49
When I tell this story I can't control the tears I shed –
and why shouldn't I weep for you, Troy, when all is said?   51
But now the hour of sleep tells us to rest and go to bed.

10

The ten-years' war had come   to an end; Ulysses, sailing home,
had stopped and moored his ship   to a rock; he'd had a close
          escape,
this hero, although so   powerful against misfortune's blows:
only the gods could beat   a man not subject to defeat.   4
So, damaged but unconquered   by the effects of heaven's hatred,
unconquered although damaged,   throughout the many years he'd
          voyaged:
he had seen Ethiops,   and Arabs, and greedy Cyclopes.

8 Et iam maioris   hominis virtute laboris
   annus erat decimus   et mensis in ordine primus:
   cum male iam fractus   et penis pene subactus
   ultima scitari   vult Tyresiamque precari.
12 Nonam post hyemem   religant cum fune biremen
   ad cautem caute   bona nacti littora naute.
   Ductor adit Thebas,   ubi tunc, vir docte, docebas
   morem vivendi,   quid dictent fata, parent di.
16 Dux quasi nauta pedes   ad vatis devenit edes,
   edes vicinis   monstrantibus ut peregrinis.
   Intrat et implorat   et vatem pronus adorat:
   'Maxime, dic, vates,   patriosne videbo penates
20 vel penitus fatum   vetat hoc? Refer, optime vatum.
   Dic, si Laertes   pater est natusque superstes;
   interpres superum,   de coniuge dic michi verum.
   Plus erit inde levis   perstans mea pena tot evis,
24 cum fuero certus.'   Sic fatur. At ille misertus
   pronum devolvit,   humilem levat, os ita solvit:
   'Novi re vera,   quid dictent fata severa,
   et quecumque Jovi   precognita sunt, ego novi;
28 verax nec quicquam   mentitus in ordine dicam,
   quicquid scire voles.   Vivit pater et tua proles,
   Telemacus,   quem pascit acus,   vivitque labore.
   Penelopem   cernes inopem   vetulamque dolore.
32 Vivit mendica,   quia maluit esse pudica.
   Si fieret mecha,   non esset inops apotheca,
   natus haberet equos.   Modo vivit acu, quia mechos
   mater contempsit.   Set malo, quod esuriens sit,
36 quam foret immunde   meretrici victus habunde.
   Perdidit armentum   pecudesque, domus alimentum,
   a mechis centum   corpus lucrata redemptum;
   perdidit omne pecus,   quod sustulit advena mechus,
40 obtinuitque decus.   Sed, qui hostis erat, foret equus
   et blandus fieret,   fieri si blanda valeret.
   Paupertate premi   sua malebat quia demi,
   quam sua cum scortis   sors esset, femina fortis
44 nunc algore, siti   morietur, amore mariti.
   Justitie zelo   fuge, redde manum cito velo,
   nos animum celo.'   Sic pectore fatus anelo,
   reddens se lecto,   iubet hunc excedere tecto.
48 Pronior ille cadens   et humum cum poplite radens

And now this was the first   month of the tenth year that had passed   8
in his ordeal – beyond   the endurance of a man to stand –
when he, already battered   by suffering and almost shattered,
decided to consult   Tiresias and learn his fate.
After the ninth winter   the sailors came to a safe harbour   12
and carefully tied up   the ship to a rocky spur with rope.
Ulysses then arrived   at Thebes, where the sage in those days gave
advice on conduct and   on what the fates or gods had planned.
On foot the leader came,   like a sailor, to the prophet's home   16
(some neighbours round about,   strangers, had pointed the place
     out),
went in, bowed down before   the seer and in this way implored:
'Great prophet, tell me, please: shall I ever see my native place,
or does fate forbid it   utterly? Answer, noble prophet.   20
And has my son survived?   Is Laertes, my father, still alive?
You speak on the gods' behalf: tell me the truth about my wife.
If I could just be sure   it would be easier to endure
my years of agony.'   At this Tiresias took pity,   24
lifted the prostrate man   to his feet again, and thus began:
'It's true, I can relate   what has been planned by cruel fate;
and all that is to be –   foreknown by Zeus – is known to me.
Without the least deception   I'll truthfully answer your questions   28
in sequence. To begin,   your father's living, and your son
Telemachus: his food   is chaff, and he lives by working hard.
Penelope, your wife,   you'll find is poor and aged by grief.
She lives in poverty   because she's chosen chastity.   32
If she'd become a whore   she'd have no lack of food in store,
and your son would have horses –   who now, since Penelope
     despises
her suitors, lives on chaff.   But better not to eat enough
than to become a dirty   prostitute and have food in plenty.   36
She lost what used to keep   the household – herds of cattle and
     sheep –
to keep her body's honour   protected from the hundred suitors;
with every sheep or ox   those lechers grabbed out of her flocks
her glory gained more ground.   If she were willing to be kind   40
her enemies would turn   to friends, and they'd be kind in turn.
She'd rather be oppressed   by want, and lose what she possessed,
that stoop to prostitution;   but now she may, courageous woman,
die from cold and thirst and   loyal love for you, her husband.   44
Hurry, and hoist your sail   to ensure that justice will prevail.

asperius meret,   quod femina panis egeret,
quam pro Telemaco,   quem vix tegit inguina sacco.
Plorat, sed gaudet   neque vult monstrare nec audet
52 vir bene precinctus,   que gaudia mens habet intus.
Jam non pressure   paupertatisque future
nec pelagi meminit: rumor bonus omnia finit
de muliere bona,   quia spreverit omnia dona
56 res precio prona,   preciosa digna corona,
cum precium reicit.   Tunc secum talia dicit:
'Jam depone metus,   iam desine fundere fletus
et lacrimas sicca,   socia vivente pudica!
60 Vela cito repara,   fac fumet Palladis ara!
Sors tua preclara,   iam nec gravis est nec amara,
dum sit avis rara   mulier pauper nec avara.
Spernere iam Venerem   nec posse capi mulierem
64 aut irretiri   pretio dampnisve feriri
vel prece molliri   prius est dyademate Cyri.
Non aurum, lapides   nec mille talenta michi des:
vincit pura fides,   quicquid dare posset Atrides;
68 plus animum sanctum   probo quam gazas Garamantum.
Miror, quod tantum   potuit, tot ut una precantum
vitarit nexus,   monitis levis obvia sexus.
Nec commota minis   neque vi nec fracta ruinis,
72 nec, dum vicinis   vicium negat, illa rapinis
nec blandimentis   ruit alta femina mentis:
iusticie miles,   vires transgressa viriles.
Nunc habitans villam   sibi suscitat ipsa favillam;
76 non habet ancillam,   que pro se suscitet illam.
Taliter oppresse   foret huic opus atque necesse
nos intrare rates.   Sed dic prius, optime vates:
credo quod, ut dicis,   redeo reddendus amicis;
80 sed quis erit ludus,   cum nudos videro nudus?
Ibo dolens Ithacam,   nec habens vitulam neque vaccam
et bibiturus aquam?   Sed mallem visere Tracam
hos gestans pannos   aut Persas sive Britannos,
84 quam miser ire domum,   cui nec seges est neque pomum
nec caro nec vinum   nec lane meis neque linum.
Nec mea me virtus   redimit, quin turpis et hirtus
quemlibet implorem,   michi qui deberet honorem,

71–2 Not in B.

Now I shall turn my thinking   to heaven.' So, out of breath with talking,
the sage dismissed the man   and lay down on his bed again.
Then, bowing, Ulysses   sank to the ground, and on his knees   48
complained more bitterly   because his wife was going hungry
than for his son and heir   with scarcely a loincloth left to wear.
He wept, and yet rejoiced,   but dared not openly express
the secret joy he harboured   now that he felt so reassured.   52
He quite forgot to dread   the thought of poverty ahead
or danger on the seas: all was dispelled by this good news
about a woman's virtue   and all the gifts she had said 'No' to.
A woman who turns down   a bribe deserves a precious crown   56
(so prone to bribery   is their sex); then he said inwardly:
'Now cast away your fears,   and now stop weeping: dry your tears;
you have a faithful wife,   and one who is alive and safe.
Quick, see to the ship's canvas   and make a sacrifice to Pallas!   60
Your fate is wonderful,   not harsh or dreadful after all;
a woman without greed,   although she's poor, is a rare bird.
A woman who rejects   the tempting blandishments of sex
and can't be beaten down   by harassment or lured by gain   64
or sweet-talked into sin   is worth more than King Cyrus's crown.
Don't give me precious stones,   or gold, or a thousand coins:
true loyalty is better   than Agamemnon's wealth could offer;
a holy mind's worth more   to me than Africa's treasure-store.   68
I wonder at her powers: ignoring all her suitors' prayers,
although her sex is frail,   alone she managed to prevail.
Resisting all compulsion,   by force or by intimidation,
resolutely opposed   to the wickedness those men proposed,   72
no flattery or force   could move her from her noble course.
She fought with all her might –   more than a man's – for what is
       right.
A cottage is her home   now, and she has to light the flame
on the hearth herself: a task   for a maid, but she has none to ask.   76
It's necessary and urgent,   since she's in this predicament,
that I should put to sea.   But first, good prophet, answer me:
when, as you recommend,   I go back home to join my friends,
what will there be to enjoy   if I'm as penniless as they?   80
Shall I go full of grief   to Ithaca, no cow or calf
to my name, and only water   to drink? Wearing these rags I'd
       rather
go off to visit Thrace,   Persia, or Britain – any place –
than go home in this state,   with neither grain nor fruit nor meat,   84

88 et me maiorem   villanum vilis adorem,
   cum pro morsello   miserabilis hostia pello,
   qui ferus in bello   castrorum claustra revello,
   assiliuntque canes,   dum quero per hostia panes,
92 cuius ad assultum   tollebat Troia tumultum,
   dum quaterem muros.   Totiens in me perituros
   excivit cives   urbs Hectore sospite dives!
   Incipiam rursus   ad cognita littora cursus,
96 esse volens ursus   vel qui setis tegitur sus?
   Malo tegi pennis,   quin desinat esse perhennis
   sudor in antennis   et iam prope pena decennis.
   Ergo responde,   – quia scis satis et potes –, unde
   perdita restaurem.   Quid enim? Citius properarem
101 patris adire larem,   nisi meque meosque iuvarem.'

11

Primas pontifici: Bene quod sapis audio dici,
et fama teste   probitas est magna penes te.
Conspicuus veste   bene cenas, vivis honeste.
Et bene si vivis   et das bene de genitivis,
ut non egrotes,   bene convenit, ut bene potes.

[1] R had originally *Bene quod audio audio dici*, with the first *audio* then corrected to a word which Meyer prints as *bibis* and McDonough as *ludis* (but this would give a false quantity to the metre.) I follow Meyer's suggested amendment to *sapis*, as the point of Primas' advice would be lost if the bishop were already drinking well.

12

Res erit archana   de pellicia veterana.
Vilis es et plana;   tibi nec pilus est neque lana.
vilis <es> et plana.   res est, non fabula vana,
quod tua germana   fuerit clamis Aureliana.
Nec pulices operit,   latebrasque pulex ubi querit,
quas quia non reperit,   ipsa reperta perit.

[3] *es*: supplied by Meyer.

nor wine to drink, nor any   wool or linen for my family.
As filthy and unshaven   as I am, I'm likely to be driven,
my standards notwithstanding,   to one who should be honouring
me, and grovel to him,   a tenant-farmer who's become   88
greater than me; now poor,   I'll ask for scraps at his front door –
I who so fiercely tore   the camp's gates open in the war;
I'll stand there on the step   begging for bread, and dogs will leap
at me, whose armed assault   caused Troy's rebellion to halt   92
when I attacked its walls.   So often that rich city called
its death-doomed men to move   against me, when Hector was alive.
Shall I set out once more   and sail to that familiar shore
while looking like a bear   or like a bristle-covered boar?   96
I'd rather go there dressed   in feathers, flying; then at least
my sailing would have ceased   (ten years of sweat); I'd be released.
So answer me; please tell –   because you can; you know it well –
how can the things I've lost   be mine again? Should I go first
to my father, if I myself   can't give my family any help?'   101

11

Primas to bishop: Sir,   you are a wise man, I hear;
and likewise, says the rumour,   you're known for honourable
    behaviour.
Your conduct's always noble,   you dress well, keep an excellent
    table.
Your life-style is correct,   and your parts are used to good effect;
then you should not omit   good drinking, if you're to stay fit.

12

You're really quite a mystery,   you fur cloak with an ancient
    history.
You're scruffy and worn thin;   you have no wool or furry skin.
You're scruffy and worn smooth.   It's no false rumour but the truth
that your close relation   must be the cloak from Orleans.
Also you don't provide   a refuge where a flea can hide;
a searching flea finds none,   is itself discovered and undone.

13

A

Me ditavit ita   vester bonus archilevita,
ditavit Boso   me munere tam precioso.

B

Ve michi mantello,   quia sum donatus asello,
vili, non bello,   quia non homini, sed homello.

14

In cratere meo   Thetis est sociata Lieo:
    sic dea iuncta deo,   sed dea maior eo.
Nil valet hic vel ea,   nisi cum fuerint pharisea
    hec duo: propterea   sit deus absque dea.
Res ita diverse,   licet utraque sit bona per se,
si sibi perverse   coeant, perdunt pariter se.

This poem appears in a number of MSS, including the Carmina Burana: some give the whole poem, some omit lines 5–6, and there are other variations. As usual I follow Meyer.

15

Vir pietatis inops, cordis plus cortice duri,
dignus cum Juda flammis Stigialibus uri
Scariothis finem det ei deus aut Palinuri!
Pene furens tremulum fregit caput obice muri.
5 Cuius vero caput? Senis et propere morituri.
Si lupus est agnum, si vim faciat leo muri,
quod decus aut precium lupus aut leo sunt habituri?
dum metuens mortem me sepius offero iuri,
auferor et rapido furor mea guttura furi.

2
10 Verba quidem sunt severa
    et videntur esse vera,
    sed nec casta nec sincera:
    non Allecto seu Megera
        hanc habent nequiciam.

13

A

Your excellent archdeacon   enriched me thus by a donation;
he who enriched me with so   valuable a gift was Boso.

B

Poor me, poor cloak: alas,   I've been presented to an ass,
an ugly, low buffoon –   not a man at all, but a poltroon.

14

In my drinking-cup   Thetis and Bacchus are mixed up,
god and goddess together,   but the goddess is the greater.
Neither has any force   unless the two can be divorced:
let's have the god alone,   without the goddess, on his own.
Two things so totally   at odds, though individually
good, when unnaturally   joined are both wasted equally.

15

A man quite lacking in charity, with a heart harder than wood,
a man fit to burn in the flames of hell as Judas did!
May the fate of Judas or Palinurus be given him by God!
In his rage he very nearly shattered a trembling head
against a wall. Whose head? An old man's who'll soon be dead.   5
If a wolf devours a lamb, or a lion is brutally hard
on a mouse, is it a glorious act? Does it bring them a reward?
Often I offered to go to law, being in mortal dread,
but then I stole away from that thief and ran for my life instead.

2
Words, indeed, can be severe   10
and true as well (so they appear),
but not honest or sincere:
no Allecto or Megera
     does such evil damage.

15 Multos fallit sacramentis
et seducit blandimentis:
nec in falsis iuramentis
nec in verbis blandientis
   habeas fiduciam.

3

20 Requirebam meum censum
et hoc fecit hunc infensum;
sed, dum vado per descensum,
si teneret apprehensum,
vir insanus extra sensum
25   iugulasset propere.
Nec pro deo nec pro sanctis
est misertus deprecantis;
sed ad vocem tribulantis
dedit deus alas plantis;
30   et sic cessit prospere.

4

Sic res erat definita
et mors michi stabilita:
si teneret me levita,
brevis esset mea vita
35   nec possem evadere.
Si non esset levis talus,
brevis esset mea salus.
Sed dum instat hostis malus,
retardavit eum palus
40   et est visus cadere.

5

Si non esset talus velox,
Primas esset velut Pelops.
Sed, qui sedet super celos,
cui cantant dulce melos
45   beatorum anime:
non concessit ius insano,
homicide, Daciano,
quod noceret veterano;
alioquin (vera cano)

He's tricked many people with   15
flattery or a lying oath;
what he swears is not the truth:
I advise you, have no faith
    in this flatterer's language.

   3   20
when I asked for what he owed me
he became most hostile to me;
and, as I went down the stairway,
if he had contrived to catch me
(so insane with fury was he)
    he'd have strangled me at once.   25
Vainly I appealed for pity
in the name of the Almighty
and the saints; but then the Deity
gave me wings; my feet grew speedy;
    I was saved from that mischance.   30

   4
As things stood my death was certain,
there's no doubt: if I'd been taken
captive by the cruel deacon
then my life would have been shortened;
    there was no escape at all.   35
If my feet had not moved swiftly
little of my life was left me;
but when he had almost caught me
a railing tripped him up and saved me
    from my foe; I saw him fall.   40

   5
If my feet had not been rapid,
Primas would have been like Pelops;
but the Lord in heaven, worshipped
on his throne by all the blessed
    spirits in sweet harmony,   45
wouldn't let that mad assassin,
that equivalent of Dacian,
hurt so elderly a person;
or (it's true, without distortion)

50   perissem celerrime.

6

Si non essent plantis ale,
satis esset michi male;
monstrum enim Stigiale
me vorasset absque sale.
55 Conputabam gradus scale,
    sed non recto numero:
unus, septem, quinque, decem,
et in vanum fundens precem.
O quam pene vidi Lethem!
60 nam tirannus minans necem
    inminebat humero.

7

Dum demitto me per scalas,
sepe clamans 'Alas! Alas!',
dedit deus plantis alas;
65 sic evasi manus malas
    cursu debilissimus.
Quam nefandum opus egit!
Contra murum me impegit,
pene caput meum fregit.
70 Nunc extorrem me collegit,
cibat pane, veste tegit
    clerus nobilissimus.

8

Proclamabam 'Heus! heus!
miserere mei deus!',
75 dum instaret hostis meus.
Eram enim ut Zacheus:
ipse velut Briareus
aut Herodes Galileus
    sive Dionisius.
80 Vix evasi triste fatum.
Nunc suscepit exulatum
regni tenens principatum

76 *eram* Meyer: *erat* R

I'd have perished instantly.   50

6
If I hadn't had winged heels
things would not have turned out well;
for that monster out of hell
would have had me for his meal
(without salt); I called the roll   55
    of steps – all out of order:
one and seven, five and ten,
pouring out my prayers in vain.
I was close to Lethe then!
For the murder-threatening man   60
    loomed behind my shoulder.

7
As I hurtled down the stairs
shouting 'Wings!' in my despair,
wings arrived: God heard my prayer;
I escaped from my destroyer   65
    by running, though so feeble.
What an evil thing he did! –
Pushed me to the wall, and would,
if he could, have smashed my head.
Now these noble priests provide   70
clothes to cover me, and bread
    to feed me in my exile.

8
I was shouting out 'Alas!
God have pity on my case!'
as my enemy came close.   75
I was rather like Zacchaeus;
he, though, was like Briareus
or like Dionysius
    or Galilean Herod.
Barely I escaped my doom;   80
now, though, exiled as I am,
Paris gives me a new home –

et regina civitatum
   nobilis Parisius.

9

85 Multi monstrum ignorantes
vix hoc credunt admirantes
et sic dicunt indignantes:
   'quis est iste dominus?
In qua fidit potestate,
90 qui de nostro bono vate,
de magistro, de Primate,
   tale fecit facinus?'

10

Cum recordor tristis hore,
qua volabam pre timore
95 et non erat locus more,
friget plenum cor horrore
nec iam credo quemquam fore,
   cui possim credere.
Adhuc ita tremo totus.
100 Non est locus tam remotus
nec amicus quisquam notus
tam fidelis tam devotus,
   in quo possim fidere.

16

Iniuriis contumeliisque concitatus
iam diu concepi   dolorem nimium.
Nunc demum rumpere   cogor silencium,
4 cernens ecclesie   triste supplicium
et cleri dedecus   atque flagicium.
Ker quant vos volez faire   d'evesche electium,
currentes queritis   intra cenobium
8 l'abe o le prior   vel camerarium,
ut cleri sit caput   gerens capucium,
cuculla iudicet   superpellicium;
et, quem deus fecit   principem omnium

---

[10] *superpellicium* ʀ; Meyer divides as *super pellicium*, but this would mean 'over a fur coat'.

queen of cities, our supreme
  capital, much honoured.

9
Many who don't know that monster   85
half-incredulously wonder,
in astonishment and anger,
  'Who is he, that creature?
What inspired him? On what basis
did he visit such a shameless   90
crime on our good poet Primas,
  our respected teacher?'

10
When I think of that grim hour
when I truly flew in fear,
with no refuge anywhere,   95
horror chills my heart; I dare
not believe I've one sincere
  friend: my confidence is lost.
Even now the terror's present.
There's no place however distant   100
and no friend however constant,
true, familiar and decent,
  I can bring myself to trust.

16

Violently moved by injuries and insults
I have for a long time   cherished a grievance;
but now I'm compelled   at last to break silence,
seeing the Church's   terrible suffering   4
and the clergy's disgraceful   behaviour and infamy.
For whenever you want   to elect a new bishop
you run around searching   the monastic community
for an abbot or prior   or else for a chamberlain,   8
that the head of the clergy   may be one with a hood,
and the cowl be appointed   as judge of the surplice;
so the person whom God   has made chief over all

12 et ki sor toz devreit   aveir dominium,
   clericus monacho   facit hominium.
   Quem si aliquando   vidisse obvium,
   putassem vidisse   grande demonium;
16 ker le jor m'avenist   grant infortunium,
   o j'eüsse la nuit   malum hospicium.
   Vos fratrem linquitis   et intra gremium
   matris ecclesie   nutritum filium.
20 Ce fait invidia,   servile vicium,
   que stridet, non ridet,   cum videt   provehi socium.
   Or est venuz li moines   ad episcopium,
   pallidus et macer   propter ieiunium:
24 sed mox assiduo   stridore dentium
   sex frusta devorans   magnorum piscium,
   in cena consumens   ingentem lucium,
   inpinguatur ingrassatur   infra biennium,
28 porcorum exemplo   rebus carencium.
   In claustro solitus   potare fluvium,
   ore fait de forz vins   tantum diluvium,
   que l'on le porte el lit   par les braz ebrium.
32 Ore verrez venir   milia milium,
   de parenz, de nevoz   turbam, dicencium:
   je sui parenz l'evesche,   de sa cognatium.
   Dunt fait cestui canoine,   hunc thesaurarium;
36 cil, ki servierant   per longum spacium,
   amittunt laborem   atque servicium.
     Tristis hypocrita,   quem vos eligitis,
   adeptus honorem   non suis meritis,
40 primitus apparet   et bonus et mitis;
   omnibus inclinat   cervicem capitis,
   paratus prestare,   si quid exigitis.
   Sed primis duobus   annis preteritis
44 iam ferus apparet   et sevus subditis,
   vexat vos et gravat   causis et placitis.
   Secedit ad villas   in locis abditis;
   quant est priveement   et in absconditis,
48 carnibus utitur   regula vetitis.
   Si poscat rabies   lascivi capitis
   et presto sit puer,   filius militis,

---

[27] *ingrassatur = CL incrassatur.*

and who ought to have power   to rule all the people –   12
the priest, that's to say –   gives a monk his obeisance.
If ever I'd happened   to see such a person
I should have imagined   I saw a great devil;
for I should, on that day,   have met with great evil,   16
or have had, on that night,   a very bad lodging.
You abandon your brother,   you abandon the son
whom Mother Church nourished   and fed at her bosom.
It brings about envy,   a vice fit for servants,   20
which gives hisses, not smiles,   at a brother's preferment.
Now this very monk,   when he came to be bishop,
was pallid and lean   on account of his fasting:
but soon by assiduous   gnashing of teeth,   24
by swallowing helpings   of six massive fishes,
by consuming entire   a huge pike at one sitting,
in the space of two years   he becomes fat and bloated,
in the fashion of pigs   who've been kept short of food.   28
In the cloister his practice   was just to drink water,
but now he pours out   such a flood of strong wines
that they drag him off drunk   by his arms to his bed.
Now you'll see coming   a crowd of relations   32
and nephews, in thousands   of thousands, declaring
'I'm the bishop's relation,   I'm one of his kinsfolk'.
Then he makes one a canon,   another a treasurer;
and those who for ages   had held these positions   36
are relieved of their work   and dismissed from their jobs.
    The solemn-faced hypocrite   whom you've elected,
acquiring this honour   not by his own merits,
in the first place appears   to be kindly and gentle;   40
he lowers his head   to all in humility,
and whatever you want   he's prepared to provide.
But as soon as his first   two years have gone by
it's clear that he's cruel   and harsh to subordinates;   44
he chivvies and grinds you   with lawsuits and cases.
He takes himself off   to a country retreat;
and there when he's hidden   in private seclusion
he does what is banned   by the rule: he eats meat.   48
If ever he's urged   by the rage of his passions,
and if there's a boy,   the son of a knight,

que il deit adober   pro suis meritis,
52 qui virgam suscitet   mollibus digitis
    plus menu que moltun   hurte des genitis
       Tunc primum apparet   vestra dementia,
    quando pontificis   incontinentia
56 et vanitas patet   et avaritia,
    in quibusdam folie   et ignorantia.
    Caveat deinceps   Belvacus talia!
    Si quando venerit   res necessaria,
60 eslizez prode clerc   de turba socia;
    mandetur filio   mater ecclesia,
    ut mater filii   sit in custodia.
    Tunc cessent inter vos,   si qua sunt odia,
64 et latens invicem   malivolencia.
    Nel di pas por cestui: assez buen home i a.
    Bien set corteissement   faire scutilia
    et manches de coltels   atque fusilia
68 et marmosez de fust   et his similia.
       Hoc bene previdit   urbs Senonensium
    et plebis et cleri   sanum consilium,
    ki melz voldrent eslire   fidelem filium
72 quam querere foris   advenam alium.
       Mais un vasal i out,   qui, gerens baculum,
    habere voluit   mitram et anulum
    et grandem dedisset   nummorum cumulum;
76 nam vasis aureis   honerasset mulum,
    ut posset ascribi   numero presulum.
       Cil, ki primam vocem   out en l'eslectium,
    ut vir magnanimus   reiecit precium,
80 turpis simonie   devitans vicium:
    elegit et cepit   honestum socium,
    cleri leticiam,   amorem civium.
    In eo convenit   voluntas omnium,
84 neque scisma fuit   neque discidium.
    Molt m'a del suen done;   trestuit l'en mercium;
    je fui l'altrier a Senz   entor l'ascensium;
    nec fui spacio   duorum mensium.
88 Unques n'oi in mundo   si buen hospicium.
    Kis mun seignor Reinalt,   virum propicium.
    Si vellem dicere   dulce servicium.
    duorum scilicet   adolescencium,

whom he must 'invest'   on account of his merits,
this man who arouses   his rod with soft fingers   52
will outdo a ram   in his sexual assaults.
   Your folly by then   will at last be apparent,
when the uncontrolled lust   of the bishop's revealed,
and together with this   his greed and his vanity,   56
his crazy behaviour,   his lack of good sense.
Let Beauvais be on guard   against this kind of thing!
Whenever the post   may fall vacant again,
elect a good priest   from within your own circle;   60
entrust Mother Church   to the care of a son;
let one of her sons   be in charge of his mother.
Then let any malice   or mutual hostility
that's lurking among you   be brought to an end.   64
I'm not speaking of *him*:   he's a good enough man,
accomplished at making   ingenious sculptures
and handles for knives   and cast-metal images
and carved wooden gargoyles   and things of that nature.   68
   The city of Sens,   its people and clergy,
made a sensible plan   and looked wisely ahead;
they preferred to elect   a son who was faithful
and not to go searching   for a stranger abroad.   72
But a certain young man   with his own staff of office
had a wish for a mitre   and episcopal ring,
and would have presented   a large heap of coins;
he'd have given a mule   a gift of gold plate   76
if the animal could   have made him a bishop.
   The person who had   first say in the ballot
rejected the bribe, as   a man of integrity,
avoiding the vice of   infamous simony;   80
he proposed as his choice   a virtuous colleague,
a joy to the clergy   and loved by the citizens.
For this man's election   the vote was unanimous
and lacking in any   dissension or schism.   84
He gave me rich presents,   for which we all thank him;
I was recently there,   on a visit to Sens,
at the time of Ascension,   for nearly two months.
I have never enjoyed   a better reception.   88
I called on Lord Rainault,   a man well-disposed to me.
I wish I could tell you   how kindly they treated me –
the pair of young men   to whom I'm referring –

92 vestes et caligas   michi trahencium!
Nec erant pilosi   more bidencium,
nec murmur resonans   contradicencium.
Fuge suspicari   par mal intencium!
96 In hoc servicio   non fuit vicium;
etas enim mea   vergit in senium.
Archidiaconus   cepit consilium;
apela Johannem   consiliarium:
100 'Mei covient al Primat   a faire auxilium;
ker il despendra molt   ad hoc consilium.'
Avant m'aveit done   unum pellicium:
un cheval me dona,   bonum cursorium,
104 pinguem et iuvenem,   ambulatorium,
ne clop ne farcimos   neque trotarium.
Equitem remisit   meum mancipium.
   (N)unc laudem dicamus   precelso iuveni,
108 iuveni corpore,   sed moribus seni!
Nostra Calliope,   nunc michi subveni,
ne laudem deteram   ob culpam ingeni
et iram incurram   dulcis et sereni,
112 et munus merear   avene et feni.
   Dicam de maximo   iuvenum iuvene:
opem ferte michi,   Clio, Melpomene!
Docte vos forsitan   detinet Athene
116 et delectabiles   poetarum cene;
sed, que vos retinent,   laxentur catene.
Cetere sex ibi   maneant Camene:
vos autem, que turbe   principes novene,
120 nostre principium   date cantilene,
ut cantare queam   de domino bene,
ne mandare semen   videar harene.
Certus sum de dono   prandii vel cene,
124 sed adhuc de dono   dubius avene.
   (T)unc respondit unus de turba:
'Re vera semen sterili conmittis harene.
Tu enim cantabis   dulcius Sirene,
128 dulcius Orpheo   seu cigno sene,
delectabilius   voce philomene,
et eloquentior   eris Origene,

---

[101] *consilium* R; Meyer alters to *concilium*, unnecessarily.

who brought me as presents   some shoes and some clothing!   92
They weren't shaggy-bearded   and woolly as sheep,
nor did they grumble   and noisily argue.
But don't be suspicious,   mistrusting my motives!
The kindness they offered   was nothing but innocent;   96
my age, after all, is   verging on elderly.
The archdeacon pondered   and made a decision;
he sent for Johannes,   who was his counsellor:
'I need to supply some   assistance to Primas;   100
for he will depend   a good deal on this plan.'
In the past he had given me   a cloak lined with fur;
this time he gave me   a horse, a swift courser,
well-nourished and youthful,   an excellent saddle-horse,   104
not lame, not infested   with worms, not a plodder.
He sent my servant   home as a rider.
    Now let us all praise   this outstanding young man –
physically young, but   mature in his manners!   108
Now come to assist me,   my own dear Calliope,
lest my praise should fall short   through a failure of talent
and his noble illustrious   lordship be angry;
let me merit a present   of oats and of hay.   112
    I shall speak of the finest   young man in the world:
help me, support me,   Clio, Melpomene!
Perhaps you're delayed by   the culture of Athens
and by the delectable   feasts of the poets;   116
but please let the chains that   retain you be loosened.
The other six Muses   are free to stay there:
but you, who are chief   in the chorus of Nine,
give me some opening   lines for my poem,   120
so that I may sing well   in this ode to my master,
and not seem to scatter   my seed on the sand.
I am sure of his gifts   of breakfast and dinner,
but not yet assured   that he'll give me some hay.   124
    Then someone answered from the crowd:
'You are certainly sowing your seed on barren sand.
For your song will be sweeter   than that of a Siren,
sweeter than Orpheus   or a swan near to death,   128
more charming by far than   the voice of the nightingale,
and your eloquence will   surpass that of Origen,

cum tibi dabuntur   due mine plene.
132 Se je bien le conui –'
   'Frater, tu mentiris   et non dicis bene.
   Nam carmen proferam   tam pium, tam lene,
   quod vobis madebunt   pietate gene.
136 Ne quid stulte dicam,   Iesu, tu me tene!'
     Dicatur iuveni: Gloria iuvenum,
   pauperum adiutor   et baculus senum,
   Primatem procurat   pauperem, egenum,
140 annum iam agentem   plus quam quinquagenum.
   Il me fesist grant bien   ad unguem, ad plenum,
   s'il me volsist doner   avenam et fenum.
   Seignors, ker li preiez   propter Nazarenum
144 quod ipse dignetur prestare   avenam et fenum.
   Andriu l'a done il,   ki n'a plen son penum,
   et i'en ai mis en gage   et sellam et frenum.
     Mais mis sire Richarz,   quem misit Anglia,
148 super me commotus   misericordia:
   'Non est', ait, 'virtus,   sed est socordia;
   nec habent hunc morem   in nostra patria,
   quod dives prebeat   clerico prandia,
152 equus non habeat   nocte cibaria.'
   Dona mei un fustainne   et vadimonia
   insuper redemit.
155 Cui sit gloria   et gratia   et copia
   omnium bonorum   per secula seculorum.

17

Alta palus, mea parva salus etasque senilis
   me remanere iubent et via difficilis.
Ecce cavat terram sonipes pede parvus acuto;
4   vix retinere potest ungula fixa luto.
Quod si me tecum iubeas equitare, gravabor,
   decrepitumque senem conteret iste labor.
Vestra quidem bonitas vestrum ditabit amicum:
8   sed requiescenti sufficeret modicum.

when once you've been given   two measures well-filled.
If I know him well – '   132
'Brother,you're lying,   what you say isn't right.
I shall offer a song   that's so gracious and tender
that your cheeks will be wet   with noble emotions.
Lord Jesus, don't let me   say anything foolish!'   136
   Let the message be this: May the splendid young man,
kind friend of the poor   and support of the old,
be mindful of Primas,   who is poor and in need,
whose fiftieth year has   already gone by.   140
He would give me great blessing,   full up, running over,
if he cared to present me   with some oats and some hay.
So my lords, please entreat him   for the sake of our Saviour,
to deign to present me himself   with some oats and some hay.   144
He gave some to Andrew,   whose storehouse is full of it,
whereas I've had to pawn   my saddle and bridle.
   My lord Richard, however,   a native of England,
said to me, feeling his   heart moved by sympathy,   148
'That isn't good conduct   but culpable negligence;
it isn't the custom   at home in my country
that a rich man provides   a cleric with sustenance
but a horse, when day's over,   has nothing to eat.'   152
He gave me a jerkin,   and the things I had pawned
he redeemed and gave back.
To him be glory   and thanks and abundance   155
of all kinds of riches   for ever and ever.

17

Deep mud, the hazards of the road, my feeble health, all urge
that I should stay at home – these things and my advancing age.
Look how my little horse's feet are digging up the path;
his hooves can hardly keep a foothold on the slippery earth.   4
If you command me to ride out with you I shall be pained:
a task like that will wear a poor old man into the ground.
Of course, your kindness will reward your friend with a rich present;
but if I stayed at home a modest one would be sufficient.   8

18

Ambianis, urbs predives,
quam preclaros habes cives,
quam honestum habes clerum!
4 Si fateri velim verum,
sola rebus in mundanis
hoc prefulges, Ambianis,
quod nec clerum nec pastorem
8 usquam vidi meliorem.
Quam sis plena pietate,
est ostensum in Primate.
Pauper eram, spoliatus;
12 apparebat nudum latus;
spoliarat me latronum
seva manus et predonum.
Et qui erant hi latrones?
16 Deciani tabulones.
Nil habentem in crumena
remisisti bursa plena.
Ergo Remis, civitatum
20 prima tenens principatum,
tibi mandat per Primatem,
quod te facit optimatem,
ut sis una de supremis,
24 digna proles sacre Remis.
Tanta matri, tam preclare,
obedire, supplicare,
caput suum exaltare:
28 illud erit imperare;
tantam matrem venerari:
illud erit dominari.
Remis enim per etatem
32 primam tenet dignitatem:
sed, quod habet ab antiquo,
nunc augetur sub Albrico.
Per hunc Remis urbs suprema,
36 per hunc portat diadema;
per hunc fulget in corona.
Quam conmendant multa bona:
sed pre cunctis hanc divine

18

Amiens, how truly noble,
wealthy city, are your people,
and how honourable your clergy!
If I am to speak out truly,   4
your remarkable distinction
in among the world's corruption
is that I have nowhere met a
priest or bishop who was better.   8
You displayed your store of kindness
amply to myself, to Primas.
I was poor, and stripped of clothing –
yes, my naked back was showing;   12
I'd been robbed by thieves and brigands
who assaulted me with violence.
And who were they, then, these robbers?
They were dedicated gamblers.   16
You, though, when my purse was empty,
sent me on my way with plenty.
Therefore Reims, which holds high office
as the first among our cities,   20
bids Primas tell of your promotion
to the highest situation;
you will have exalted stature,
holy Reims's worthy daughter.   24
To obey and beg for favour
from so excellent a mother,
and to lift her head to heaven:
this is how you are to govern;   28
by your rule you must give honour
to the greatness of your mother.
Reims has held throughout the ages
foremost rank among the cities;   32
now, though, her time-hallowed status
is enhanced by Albericus.
Through this man she stands unequalled;
through this man she wears a jewelled   36
crown; a diadem adorns her.
Many good things recommend her
but above all else her holy

40 fons illustrat discipline,
    fons preclarus atque iugis,
    fons doctrine non de nugis,
    non de falsis argumentis,
44 sed de Christi sacramentis.
    Non hic artes Marciani
    neque partes Prisciani,
    non hic vana poetarum:
48 sed archana prophetarum,
    non leguntur hic poete:
    sed Iohannes et prophete;
    non est scola vanitatis:
52 sed doctrina veritatis;
    ibi nomen non Socratis:
    sed eterne trinitatis;
    non hic Plato vel Thimeus:
56 hic auditur unus deus;
    nichil est hic nisi sanctum.
    Sed in scolis disputantum
    sunt discordes et diversi,
60 aberrantes et dispersi:
    quod hic negat, ille dicit;
    hic est victus, ille vicit;
    doctor totum contradicit.
    Nos concordes super idem
65 confitemur unam fidem,
    unum deum et baptisma.
    Non hic error neque scisma,
    sed pax omnis et consensus;
69 hinc ad deum est ascensus.
    Ergo iure nostra scola
    singularis est et sola.
    Scolam dixi pro doctrina:
73 o mutare possum in a
    et quam modo dixi scolam,
    iam habentem Christi stolam,
    apellare volo scalam.
77 Hic peccator sumit alam,
    alam sumit, ut ascendat,
    ut ad deum volans tendat.
    Hic fit homo dei templum.

spring of learning brings her glory –   40
flowing brilliant and perpetual,
fed by doctrine, not by trivial
details or false arguments
but by the Christian sacraments.   44
Not here the arts of Martianus
or the parts of Priscianus
or the trifling stuff of poets:
just the mysteries of the prophets.   48
People here don't read the poets
but John's Gospel and the prophets.
This is not a school for vanities;
here they lecture on the verities,   52
not in the name of Socrates
but in the eternal Trinity's.
Here's there's no Platonic teaching:
one true God is all the preaching.   56
All that's here is true religion.
But in schools of disputation
there is argument and discord;
some have strayed and some are scattered;   60
what some state the others counter;
someone's vanquished, someone's victor;
all's refuted by the teacher.
We agree, though, on one doctrine;
here one faith is our confession,   65
one true God and one baptism.
There's no heresy or schism;
all is harmony and concord;
here the way to God leads upward.   69
So it can be said with justice
that our school's unique and peerless.
'School', I called it, since it teaches;
but if just one letter changes,   73
making 'scala' out of 'scola',
then our school – which has the stola
of our Lord – becomes a ladder.
Here there's upward flight: the sinner   77
takes on wings to rise up skyward,
flying to approach the Godhead.
Here a man becomes a temple.

81 Prope satis est exemplum:
    ecce noster Fredericus
    comes comis et amicus,
    et cum eo Adelardus
85 valde dives Longobardus;
    generosus puer Oto
    et quam plures pari voto
    hic aggressi viam vite
89 sacri degunt heremite;
    per hanc scolam sursum tracti
    sunt celorum cives facti;
    hoc preclaro fonte poti
93 modo deo sunt devoti.
    Vos, doctrinam qui sititis,
    ad hunc fontem qui venitis
    audituri Iesum Christum,
97 audietis furem istum?
    In conventu tam sacrato
    audietur iste Gnato?
    Dignus risu vel contemptu,
101 cur hoc sedes in conventu?
    Nunc legistis Salomonem:
    audietis hunc latronem?
    Nunc audistis verbum dei:
105 audietis linguam rei?
    Reus est hic deprehensus,
    verberatus et incensus.
    Quod apparet in cocturis,
109 que sunt signa capti furis.
    Quantum gula sit leccatrix,
    nonne signat hec cicatrix?
    Revertatur ad cucullam
113 et resumat vestem pullam:
    aut videbo rursus coqui,
    nisi cesset male loqui;
    aut discedat aut taceto
117 vel iactetur in tapeto.

Close at hand there's an example: 81
look at Frederic, our kind
colleague and obliging friend;
then with him there's Adelard
(very wealthy – he's a Lombard);   85
and young Otto, nobly born,
and the rest who've likewise sworn
to pursue the Way of Life as
hermits in God's holy service;   89
through this school such men have risen
to be citizens of Heaven;
when they've drunk at this great fountain
only God has their devotion.   93
You who thirst for holy doctrine,
you who come here to this fountain
eager to hear Christ our Saviour,
will you listen to this robber?   97
In this school of sacred learning
shall this Gnatho get a hearing?
Shall a man who's earned derision
and scorn sit here as our companion?   101
You've been reading Solomon:
will you listen to this villain?
You've been hearing God's own word:
shall a convict's voice be heard?   105
Yes, a convict: one arrested
for a crime, and whipped and branded.
Look! His branded marks are proof
that the man's a captured thief.   109
Can't you see the scar, a token
showing he's a greedy glutton?
Let him wear a cowl once more,
and a dark habit, as before;   113
or again I'll see him branded,
if his evil talk's not ended;
let him either leave, or stop it,
or be tossed up in a blanket.   117

19

Egregius dedit hanc iuvenis clamidem sine pelle.
Non habuit pellem; sed habebat nobile velle.

20

A

Auxilio pellis clades inimica puellis
carnem non angit nec avis me sordida tangit.

B

Nec pulices ledunt, quia pelle vetante recedunt,
nec culices timeo, velante caput conopeo.

21

A ducibus Primas petiit duo dona duobus,
    ut duo dona probent, quam sit uterque probus.

22

Dels ego: quinque tulit solidos mulier peregrina,
et merito, quia grande tulit pondus resupina.

23

Dives eram et dilectus
inter pares preelectus:
modo curvat me senectus
4   et etate sum confectus.
Unde vilis et neglectus
a deiectis sum deiectus,
quibus rauce sonat pectus,
8   mensa gravis pauper lectus,
quis nec amor nec affectus,
sed horrendus et aspectus.

---

[1] *Dels ego: quinque* Meyer. ʀ has < >*els ego. v.* Meyer reads <#>*els.*

19

An excellent young man gave me this cloak. It isn't lined:
he had no fur, but he had a noble purpose in mind.

20

A

A fur coat's a shield: it keeps girls from being defiled
by carnal attacks, and guards   me from being shat on by birds.

B

Flea-bites are no bother: they can't get at me through the leather;
and gnats don't make me quail: I'm wearing netting as a veil.

21

Primas asked two princes for two gifts: a dual request
so that each could show his character was of the best.

22

I got only two shillings; the foreign woman got a crown.
Fair enough: she had a heavy load to bear when she lay down.

23

I was rich, and people loved me;
there was none they set above me;
now decrepitude has bent me
and old age has quite undone me.   4
So I'm poor, and they neglect me;
even down-and-outs reject me −
those whose chests resound with coughing,
who sleep rough and feed on offal,   8
those who live unloved and friendless,
whose appearance is horrendous.

Homo mendax atque vanus
12 infidelis et profanus
me deiecit capellanus
veteranum veteranus
et iniecit in me manus
16 dignus dici Dacianus.
Prius quidem me dilexit
fraudulenter et illexit.
Postquam meas res transvexit,
20 fraudem suam tunc detexit.
Primas sibi non prospexit
neque dolos intellexit,
donec domo pulsus exit.
Satis erat bonus ante
25 bursa mea sonum dante
et dicebat michi sancte:
'Frater, multum diligam te.'
Hoc deceptus blandimento,
29 ut emunctus sum argento,
cum dolore, cum tormento
sum deiectus in momento,
32 rori datus atque vento.
Vento datus atque rori,
vite prima turpiori
redonandus et errori;
36 pena dignus graviori
et ut Judas dignus mori,
qui me tradens traditori
dignitatem vestri chori
40 tam honesti tam decori
permutabam viliori.
Traditori dum me trado,
qui de nocte non est spado,
44 me de libro vite rado
et, dum sponte ruens cado,
est dolendum quod evado.
Inconsulte nimis egi;
48 in hoc malum me inpegi.
Ipse michi collum fregi,

---

12   After this line Meyer inserts from P '*plus avarus quam Romanus*', not in R.

   A deceitful man, a vain man,
and a faithless and profane man   12
threw me out: it was the chaplain,
old himself, who laid rough hands on
me, a similarly old man.
He deserves the name of Dacian.   16
   In the past he doted on me,
led me on and slyly conned me.
When he'd stripped me of my assets
he revealed less pleasant facets.   20
Primas, innocent and guileless,
didn't spot this crooked practice
till the man had made him homeless.
   He was kind, as I recall it,
when I had a chinking wallet.   25
Sanctimoniously he'd murmur
'I'm so fond of you, dear brother!'
   This sweet talking won me over;
but when I ran out of silver   29
then in misery and torture
I was thrown out helter-skelter
to endure the winds and weather.   32
   To the weather I was given,
and a life of degradation;
back to wandering I was driven.
I deserved a harsher sentence;   36
I deserved to die like Judas:
my defection to a traitor
meant I left your noble chapter,
with its dignity, and honour,   40
for a life that's far inferior.
   Going over to that traitor –
who's no eunuch after nightfall –
scratched me from the book of life; for   44
I ran headlong to my downfall.
That I got away is shameful.
   It was far too rash an action;
I contrived my own destruction,   48
gave my own neck to be broken,

qui vos linquens preelegi,
ut servirem egro gregi,
52 vili malens veste tegi,
quam servire summo regi,
ubi lustra tot peregi.
    Aberravi: sed pro deo
56 indulgete michi reo!
Incessanter enim fleo,
pro peccato gemens meo.
    Fleo gemens pro peccatis,
60 iuste tamen et non gratis;
et non possum flere satis,
vestre memor honestatis
et fraterne karitatis.
64 o quam dura sors Primatis,
quam adversis feror fatis!
Segregatus a beatis,
sociatus segregatis,
68 vestris tantum fidens datis,
pondus fero paupertatis.
    Paupertatis fero pondus;
meus ager, meus fundus,
72 domus mea totus mundus,
quem pererro vagabundus.
Quondam felix et fecundus
et facetus et facundus,
76 movens iocos et iocundus,
quondam primus, nunc secundus
victum quero verecundus.
    Verecundus victum quero.
80 Sum mendicus. Ubi vero
victum queram nisi clero,
enutritus in Piero,
eruditus sub Homero?
84 Sed dum mane victum quero
et reverti cogor sero,
iam in brevi (nam despero)
87 onerosus vobis ero.
    Onerosus et quo ibo?
89 ad laicos non transibo.
Parum edo, parum bibo.

when I left your congregation
and defected to a sick one –
chose rough clothes, rather than stay on   52
here, and serve the King of Heaven
where for many years I had done.
    God's my judge, I was in error;
but have mercy on this sinner!   56
Now I weep without remission,
sighing over my transgression.
    Yes, I weep for my transgressions –
rightly, though, and with good reason;   60
I can hardly weep enough, when
I remember all your virtues
and fraternal acts of kindness.
Oh, how cruel is Primas' portion!   64
What adversity I'm plunged in –
cast out from the blessed brethren
and with outcasts for companions,
trusting only in your charity   68
to relieve the weight of poverty.
    Poverty's the weight I carry:
now my farm, my patrimony
and my home are scattered over   72
all the world where I must wander.
I was happy once, productive,
witty, verbally effective,
an amusing, cheerful fellow;   76
once I led, but now I follow,
cringing, forced to beg and borrow.
    I'm embarrassed. I'm a beggar,
cadging hand-outs. But who other   80
than the clergy should I bother –
I who had my education
from the Muses and from Homer?
But if in my desperation   84
I turn up and ask for rations
morning and evening (I've no option)
soon you'll see me as a burden.   87
    Where should I bestow this burden?
I can't go and bother laymen.   89
I eat little, I drink little;

Venter meus sine gibbo
92 et contentus pauco cibo
plenus erit parvo libo
et, si fame deperibo,
95 culpam vobis hanc ascribo.
Vultis modo causam scire,
97 causam litis, causam ire,
que coegit nos exire?
Brevi possum expedire,
100 si non tedet vos audire.

Responsio sociorum
Nos optamus hoc audire
102 plus quam sonum dulcis lyre.

Primas
Quidam frater claudo pede
104 est eadem pulsus ede
violenter atque fede,
ut captivus et pars prede
alligatus loris rede
108 a Willelmo Ganimede.

Frater membris dissolutus,
qui deberet esse tutus,
(nam pes erat preacutus),
112 nichil mali prelocutus,
sed mandata non secutus,
calciatus et indutus,
est in luto provolutus.

116 Provolutus est in luto
frater pede preacuto.
Quem clamantem dum adiuto
et putabam satis tuto,
120 fui comes provoluto
et pollutus cum polluto.

Provoluto comes fui
et in luto pulsus rui.
124 Dum pro bono penas lui,
nullus meus, omnes sui.

Adiuvabant omnes eum

---

[108] Meyer expands this to two lines, as in c; I follow ʀ.
[115] After this line Meyer inserts from ᴘ '*provolutus et pollutus*', not in other MSS.
[126] After this line Meyer inserts from ᴘ '*Jebusei Jebuseum*', not in other MSS.

there's no paunch around my middle.
I'm content with humble food –   92
a bit of pancake's all I need –
and if I should die of hunger
it's at you I'd point the finger.   95
    Would you like to know the reason
for the anger, for the friction   97
which gave rise to my expulsion?
I'll explain it briefly for you,
if to hear it wouldn't bore you.   100

    'Hearing that would please us more
than sweet music on the lyre.'   102

    Well, a brother who was lame
was ejected from the same   104
building with rough barbarism,
like a prisoner in wartime
tied up like some looted item,
by that Ganymede called William.   108
    This poor man who was disabled
and who should have been respected
(since his foot was badly crippled),
who'd said nothing to offend him   112
but had merely not obeyed him,
this man, fully clothed and shod,
was hurled down into the mud.
    Down he went, the lame man, falling   116
in the mud, and lay there calling.
Then when I went to his rescue,
thinking it was safe to do so,
I was sent to join my brother,   120
comrades in a mess together.
    Like my brother I went falling;
in the mud they pushed me headlong,
punished for my kindness to him;   124
everyone supported William.
    They were all of William's party,

Chananei Chananeum
128 Ferezei Ferezeum
et me nemo preter deum,
dum adiuto fratrem meum
nil merentem neque reum.
132   Solus ego motus flevi,
fletu genas adinplevi
ob magistri scelus sevi
et dolorem iam grandevi.
136   Quis haberet lumen siccum,
cernens opus tam iniquum,
sacerdotem inpudicum,
corruptorem meretricum,
140 matronarum et altricum,
sevientem in mendicum,
claudum senem et antiquum,
dum distractus per posticum
144 appellaret replens vicum
adiutorem et amicum?
Nec adiutor est repertus
nec sacerdos est misertus:
148 ita solus est desertus,
totus luto coopertus
nec, quo pedem ferret, certus.
Accusabam turpem actum
152 propter fratrem sic confractum,
claudum senem et contractrum:
et, dum dico 'malefactum',
accusatus dedi saltum.
156   Accusatus saltum dedi.
Post hec intus non resedi
neque bibi nec comedi
capellani iussi fedi,
160 qui, quod sacre datur edi,
aut inpertit Palamedi
aut largitur Ganimedi
aut fraterno dat heredi,
164 aut asportant cytharedi,
ut adquirat bonus credi.
Modo, fratres, iudicate
neque vestro pro Primate

Canaanites and Perrizites; he
had his fellow-tribesmen's loyalty.   128
I had only the Almighty
when I helped my far from guilty
brother in his difficulty.

    Only I was moved to weeping;   132
down my cheeks the tears were seeping
at the master's wicked cruelty
and the old lame brother's misery.

    Who could see without a tear a   136
thing so wickedly unfair: a
cleric scandalously given
to debauchery with women –
whores or matrons, nurses even –   140
mad with rage towards a beggar
and a cripple, till the latter,
old and thrown out in the gutter,
made the village echo round him,   144
shouting for a friend to help him?

    But no help could be discovered
and the priest remained hard-hearted;
so the cripple was deserted,   148
all his body mud-bespattered:
where was he to turn, he wondered.

    I denounced this vile behaviour
towards the limping, lame old brother   152
who'd been made to come a cropper.
When I told them 'This is wicked!'
I too was denounced and booted.

    Yes, denounced and booted headlong.   156
After this I lost my lodging
and my rations as a boarder
by the vicious chaplain's order.
All the money that he gathers   160
for the church's use he squanders
on his Ganymede, on gamblers,
on his nephew, on lute-players –
a device for the promotion   164
of his generous reputation.

    Now, my brothers, give your verdict!
Be quite honest on the subject;

168 aberrantes declinate
a sincera veritate:
an sit dignus dignitate
vel privandus potestate
172 senex carens castitate
et sacerdos honestate,
caritate, pietate,
plenus omni feditate,
176 qui, exclusa caritate,
nos in tanta vilitate,
quorum fama patet late,
179 sic tractavit. Judicate!

175–9 Only in H.

don't be tempted into bias   168
as a favour to your Primas.
Which is fitting: noble office
or the loss of his high status
for an old man who's a lecher   172
and a priest who lacks all honour,
Christian charity, and goodness? –
Who, replete with every foulness
and without a trace of kindness,   176
treated me with such great meanness –
me, whose fame is so resplendent
through the world. Deliver judgement!   179

Explanatory notes

Poem 1

4 Rufus: Red-haired people were believed to be treacherous by nature. The man attacked here has been identified as Arnulfus Rufus of Orléans (see B. M. Marti, 'Hugh Primas and Arnulf of Orléans', *Speculum* 30 (1955) 233–8).

35–6 In these two lines Primas abandons the end-rhymed elegiac couplet form in favour of Leonine verses, but my translation does not reflect this inconsistency.

37 Decius was the patron of gamblers.

Poem 2

23 See Genesis 27,11.

Poem 3

1 In several medieval treatments of the Orpheus story he succeeds in winning Eurydice back (see P. Dronke, 'The return of Eurydice', *CL. et Med.*, 1962). There is no way of telling how Primas ended his version, if indeed the poem is incomplete. Dronke suspects it is open-ended: Orpheus, the poet's *alter ego*, is a begging-poet, waiting to see how his patron, Pluto, will respond.

2 Orpheus was the son of Calliope.

23 The river: Acheron.

24 The boatman: Charon.

27 The king: Pluto.

33 Pluto was the brother of Jupiter and Neptune.

Poem 4

1 The poem is in two parts: a propemptikon for the poet's friend, and a comic dialogue on his own fears of sea-travel.

6 Imarus: possibly the Benedictine Imar, who became abbot of Montierneuf in Poitiers and later (1142) a cardinal.

15 *Tu autem*: part of the liturgical phrase 'Tu autem, Domine, miserere nobis', that brings the service of Compline to a close; it was thence used as a closing formula for readings after meals in monastic refectories.

Poem 5

1 Based on the story of Dives and Lazarus in Luke 16, 19–23, of which there are several echoes in the poem. Primas' heartfelt sympathy for the beggar and savage enjoyment of the rich man's fate reflect, as so often, his own emotions.

Poem 6

1 May: spring was the traditional season for love.

2 Menelaus was distressed when Paris lured Helen away from him.

16 Cyrus: king of Persia; Phraates: king of Parthia.

24 Lit. '[I] who do not want to change by deceit the flank which is familiar to me.' The translation of this passage is complicated by the fact that in English both varieties of bird are called doves.

Poem 7

1 The other side of the coin: realistic consolation for Flora's departure.

26 The new lover has paid the prostitute to let the poet go.

Poem 8

1 A further development of the prostitute theme. It is difficult, as Meyer says, to see Primas in the rich householder portrayed here. The poem is general rather than personal.

42 A man on foot: *pedes*, as contrasted with the *equites*, or knights, of a higher social class. Peleus etc. are intended to suggest men of high rank.

Poem 9

1 Meyer takes the speaker to be Ulysses, after the fall of Troy, but this is unlikely. More probably a humbler and anonymous member of the Greek forces is speaking. Curtius (*Die Musen im Mittelalter*, p.138) sees the poem as a rhetorical exercise on this well-known subject, telling the story in the persona of a Greek but breaking off at the end when he goes to bed.

16 Paris was the bad heir.
26 Ilus: the founder of Troy.
41 Our tricks: those of Ulysses and the Greeks.
42 Apollo, with the assistance of Poseidon, built the walls of Troy for Laomedon (see Ovid, *Metamorphoses*, 11, 194ff.)
48 The young general: Pyrrhus.

Poem 10

1 Meyer's suggestion that this poem and no.9 were originally parts of a longer epic is unconvincing.
14 The Latin uses the vocative; 'You, learned man,...'
30,34 The word *acus* has two distinct meanings. Meyer takes it to mean 'needle' in these two lines – i.e. Penelope earns her living, and her son's, by sewing. To interpret the word as 'chaff', with McDonough, makes better sense.
77 It is not clear at what point Ulysses ends his unspoken meditation and turns to address Tiresias again. McDonough takes this as occurring at 'Taliter...' Meyer tends to prefer 'Sed dic prius...' as the beginning of the speech. My punctuation leaves the question open.
96–101 Meyer calls this passage obscure; he believes the poem to be incomplete, but there seems no reason to agree. As P. Dronke has suggested, Primas sees his own plight in the poverty of Ulysses (sympathising particularly with the lack of wine in lines 82–5), and is using the fictional situation to emphasise his own needs.

Poem 12

4 Perhaps the cloak from poem 2.

Poem 13

2 Boso: probably the bishop of Châlons-sur-Marne 1153–62.

Poem 14

1 Thetis: a sea-nymph, signifying water. Bacchus: the god of wine; he was occasionally called Lyaeus.

Poem 15

3 Palinurus: the helmsman of Aeneas, who fell overboard and drowned (see *Aeneid* 5, 854ff.).
13 Allecto, Megera: two of the Furies.
42 Pelops: son of Tantalus, king of Phrygia; as a child he was killed and served as a meal to the gods, but was brought back to life by Jupiter.

47 Dacian: the persecutor of the martyr Vincent.

76 Zacchaeus: see Luke 19,3; Zacchaeus was 'little of stature', like Primas.

77 Briareus: a hundred-armed giant.

79 Dionysius: the tyrant of Syracuse.

92 *Magister* may also suggest his pre-eminence among poets; he is both 'teacher' and 'master'.

Poem 16

1 This line is a quotation from Sallust, *Cat.* 35,3; the assumption that it would have been familiar could excuse the fact that Primas begins his poem with a line of prose.

6 The indiscriminate mixing of Latin and Old French within one poem in this way is highly unusual; other macaronic poems of the time tended to follow a more orderly pattern.

21 The line as it stands has three extra syllables. Opinions vary as to what, if anything, should be omitted to make it regular. Ehlers (in 'Zum 16. Gedicht des Hugo von Orleans') suggests 'provehi', McDonough 'cum videt'.

25 See Matthew 8,12.

27 This line also exceeds the metre. As in line 21, the purpose is to gain an extra internal rhyme.

38 See Matthew 6,16. 'Gnashing of teeth' hints at the bishop's fate.

51-3 There has been much controversy over the meaning of these lines. In part I follow McDonough's edition (where his interpretation diverges slightly from suggestions made in his 1979 article), but he mistranslates *adober*, which = 'to arm or equip a knight'. My version of line 51 was suggested by P. Dronke.

65-8 These lines have also caused much debate. I follow McDonough, who suggests that the lines may be directed to one of the crowd. He takes the passage as an ironic reference to the fact that the man in question is a maker of idols – i.e. a pagan and not suitable for high office. He reads *fusilia* as 'images made from cast metal' and not 'spindles' (as in Meyer), and suggests that *scutilia* should be read as *sculptilia*: i.e. carved images. On *manches de coltels* (knife-handles) P. Dronke points out that the Rule of St Benedict forbids monks to keep knives on their person.

73 This does not signify that the young man was an abbot, as McDonough states; he was at most a subdeacon, who was given the *baculus* during the Feast of Fools. This feast is specially well documented for Sens and Beauvais, in E. K. Chambers, *The Medieval Stage*, I 278-89. (P. Dronke's note.)

78 Probably the dean of the chapter.

81 Hugh of Toucy, archbishop of Sens 1142-68.

91 The two young men were presumably in the service of Lord Rainault.

97 *senium* would suggest that Primas was over 70 (see Isidore, *Etymologies* IX 2); but see also line 140.

98 The archdeacon normally advised the bishop on financial matters. The various personalities involved, and their relations with one another, have led to

several conflicting interpretations of this section of the poem. I have followed McDonough's edition.

106 McDonough takes *equitem* as = *equum*, meaning 'he sent me back with a horse as my servant'. I follow Meyer's interpretation; poor though Primas made himself out to be, he would have had a clerk or servant of some kind.

109,113 Calliope was the muse of epic poetry, Clio of history, Melpomene of song.

125 See Mark 9,17. This line refers to the crowd Primas is addressing at Beauvais. Once again he abandons his metre: according to Meyer this line is prose, 126 a hexameter.

130 The Christian philosopher Origen was famous for his eloquence.

132 Opinions differ as to whether this half-line – another indication of the lively, immediate style of the piece – is to be assigned to the man in the crowd or to Primas, interrupting him. I follow McDonough in taking it as an aside by the former.

133–6 Primas' reply to the heckler.

144 This line has extra syllables in the first half.

147 The Englishman, Sire Richarz, has not been identified. A major Feast of Fools, such as that of Beauvais in the 1140s, where Primas will have first performed this piece, attracted members of the nobility as well as of the clergy from far and wide. (P. Dronke's note.)

Poem 18

1 Primas is writing a letter from Reims to his friends at Amiens. After praising their generosity he turns to the wonders of the Cathedral School at Reims.

16 *Deciani* is from Decius, the patron of gamblers; *Deciani tabulones* are his devotees, who move the pieces (*tabulae*) on the board (*tabularium*). Meyer called the word 'tabulones' a 'witty neologism' (see McDonough, 'Two poems', p. 123).

18–21 *Remisisti* plays on the sound of the word *Remis*, as does *Prima* on *Primatem*.

34 Albericus was director of the Cathedral School at Reims from about 1121 to 1136.

45 Martianus Capella, a 5th c. writer on the liberal arts.

46 Priscianus: early 6th c. grammarian. 'Parts' = parts of speech.

55 Lit. = 'Not here Plato or Timaeus'. Plato's dialogue *Timaeus* is perhaps included for the rhyme.

82–5 Frederic and Adelard cannot be identified; the Lombards were known as the bankers of Europe.

86 Otto: possibly Otto of Freising.

97 Meyer identified this man as Abelard, but others find this unlikely. There is no evidence for a sojourn of Abelard's at Reims. J.R. Williams has suggested ('Cathedral School', p.111) that he was the heretic Henry of Lausanne. No definite identification can be made. As P. Dronke notes, *istum* suggests that the

man is present at the performance, and this modifies the tone, giving it the rough humour of a 'flyting'.

99 Gnatho: the parasite in Terence's *Eunuchus*.

107–111 Criminals could be branded, but McDonough suggests ('Two poems', p. 117–18) that this might refer to trial by ordeal for either theft or heresy.

117 *tapeto* has been taken as a shroud or winding-sheet, but Curtius (*Die Musen im Mittelalter*, p.132) believes that it refers to the 'student prank' of tossing someone in a blanket.

Poem 23

16 See note to poem 15,47.

32 lit. = 'given to the dew and wind'. The phrase is inverted in line 33.

51 McDonough interprets this as 'a spiritually ill community', not a community of the sick, a hospital, as Meyer takes it. Likewise '*vili veste*' could refer to clothing which has brought dishonour to Primas by his defection to that other community, rather than to materially inferior clothing.

108 Ganymede: frequently used in medieval poetry for a homosexual; see line 43 above.

126–8 lit. = 'They all helped him, Canaanites [helping] a Canaanite, Perizzites a Perizzite.' See Exodus 23,23: the Perizzites and Canaanites worshipped other gods than Jehovah.

162 Palamedes was the inventor of dicing, and thus represents gambling.

The Archpoet

I

1 Lingua balbus, hebes ingenio,
  viris doctis sermonem facio;
  sed quod loquor, qui loqui nescio,
  necessitas est, non presumptio.

2 Ego iuxta divinum eloquium
  viris bonis hoc reor congruum,
  ut subportet magnus exiguum,
  egrum sanus, et prudens fatuum.

3 Ne sim reus et dignum odio
  si lucernam premam sub modio,
  quod de rebus humanis sentio
  pia loqui iubet intentio.

4 Brevem vero sermonem facio,
  ne vos gravet longa narracio,
  ne dormitet lector pre tedio
  et 'Tu autem' dicat in medio.

5 Ad eternam beatitudinem
  lapsum deus revocans hominem
  verbum suum, suam imaginem
  misit ad nos per matrem virginem.

6 Est unita deitas homini,
  servo suo persona domini,
  morti vita, splendor caligini,
  miseria beatitudini.

7 Scimus ista potentialiter
  magis facta quam naturaliter;
  scrutantibus spiritualiter
  scire licet quare, non qualiter.

8 Arte mira, miro consilio
  querens ovem, bonus opilio

The text is, as usual, that of Manitius (1929), but I have in some cases altered spelling and punctuation to conform with that of Peter Dronke in 'The Art of the Archpoet'. Other variants are noted as they occur.
[1.3] *quod* Wa. and Dr.; *quid* Ma.
[2.1–2] Wa. has *'Nulli vestrum reor ambiguum, / viris bonis hoc esse congruum'.*

1

Though dull of wit and prone to stammering,   1
I'm making a speech to men of learning.
What makes me speak without knowing how to
is not presumption but that I have to.

As in the words God spoke to us,   2
I think good men should behave like this:
the great man should support the small,
the healthy the sick, the wise the fool.

In case I'm thought guilty and hateful   3
for hiding my light under a bushel,
my sense of duty tells me it's needful
to speak my mind on the ways of people.

But I shall make my speech a short one,   4
and not oppress you with a long sermon,
or the lector may nod off through boredom
and, halfway through, pronounce 'Tu autem'.

Recalling fallen man to share   5
eternal felicity once more,
God sent his word to us, his image;
his virgin mother brought that message.

Godhead and man have been united,   6
the master and the slave conflated,
life joined to death, splendour to darkness,
and wretchedness to blessedness.

We know this happened not by natural   7
means but through the divine potential;
those who gaze with the spirit's eyes
may know the reason, though not the cause.

Searching for his sheep as we wandered   8
here in our exile, the good shepherd

vagantibus in hoc exilio
locutus est nobis in filio.

9 Sanctum sue mentis consilium
patefecit mundo per filium,
ut, reiecto cultu sculptilium,
deum nosset error gentilium.

10 Poetarum seductos fabulis
veritatis instruxit regulis;
signis multis atque miraculis
fidem veram dedit incredulis.

11 Obmutescant humana somnia:
nil occultum, iam patent omnia;
revelavit fata latentia
non sapiens, sed Sapientia.

12 Conticescat falsa temeritas,
ubi palam loquitur veritas;
quod divina probat auctoritas
non improbet humana falsitas.

13 Huius mundi preterit orbita;
stricta ducit ad vitam semita:
qui scrutatur renum abscondita
trutinabit hominum merita.

14 Iudex iustus, inspector cordium,
nos ad suum trahit iudicium,
redditurus ad pondus proprium
bona bonis, malis contrarium.

15 In hac vita misere vivitur,
vanitas est omne quod cernitur;
eri natus hodie moritur,
finem habet omne quod oritur.

16 Sed qui dedit ad tempus vivere
vitam brevem potest producere;
vitam potest de morte facere,
qui mortuos iubet resurgere.

17 Nos ad regna vocat celestia,
ubi prorsus nulla miseria,

with his wonderful art and plan
spoke to us in the voice of his Son.

Through his Son he clearly outlined   9
to the world the holy plan in his mind;
so that the straying pagans, the gentiles,
should know God and reject their idols.

To those seduced by the poets' tales   10
he taught instead the truth and its rules;
he gave the faith to unbelievers
by showing many signs and wonders.

Let human imaginings be silent: 11
nothing's concealed now, all is patent:
the hidden fates have been laid open
by Wisdom, not by one wise person.

Be silent, therefore, false temerity,   12
now that the truth itself speaks openly;
let what is shown by divine authority
not be rejected by human falsity.

This world's tracks will have faded tomorrow;   13
the path that leads to life is narrow.
He who can scan deep hidden regions
weighs the merits of men in his balance.

The righteous judge who ponders each heart   14
brings us to trial before his court,
to restore the balance in equality:
good to the good, to the bad the contrary.

In this life we live in misery;   15
everything we see is vanity;
the man born yesterday dies today;
all that arises passes away.

But he who made life temporary   16
can also lengthen its brevity:
he who can tell the dead to come forth
alive can make life out of death.

He calls us to the Kingdom of Heaven,   17
where truly there's no tribulation,

sed voluptas et vera gaudia,
que sit deus omnibus omnia.

18 Puniamus virtute vicium
cuius caret fine supplicium;
terreat nos ignis incendium,
fetor, fletus, et stridor dentium.

19 Sciens deus nos esse teneros,
et Gehenne dolores asperos,
pia voce revocat miseros,
ovem suam ponens in humeros.

20 O pietas inestimabilis:
omnipotens incorruptibilis,
creature misertus mobilis,
est pro nobis factus passibilis.

21 Est alapas passus et verbera,
ludicrorum diversa genera,
sputas, spinas, et, preter cetera,
crucis morte dampnatus aspera.

22 Cum creator in cruce patitur,
ferreus est, qui non conpatitur;
cum salvator lancea pungitur,
saxeus est qui non conpungitur.

23 Conpungamur intus in anima,
iram dei placantes lacrima:
dies irae, dies novissima
cito venit, nimis est proxima.

24 Ecce redit districtus arbiter
qui passus est misericorditer;
redit quidem, sed iam minaciter –
coactus est, non potest aliter.

25 Mundus totus conmotus acriter
vindicabit auctorem graviter
et torquebit reos perhenniter
quamvis iuste, tamen crudeliter.

17.4 *que* Wa. and Dr.; *quod* Ma.

but pleasure and joys that never pall,
which God will be: our all in all.

Let us use virtue as a punishment   18
for vice which earns unending torment;
we ought to dread the fire's hot breath,
the stench, the weeping and gnashing of teeth.

God, aware that we're tender creatures   19
and knowing the harshness of hell's tortures,
calls us back with loving reminders
(poor things), and sets his sheep on his shoulders.

So infinite was his devotion   20
and pity for changeable creation,
the almighty, incorruptible one
made himself able to suffer pain.

He had to suffer slaps and whipping,   21
various kinds of public mocking,
spittle and thorns; and, beyond all this,
he endured a cruel death on the cross.

Only a man of iron won't suffer   22
with the crucifixion of the Creator;
when a lance has pierced the Saviour, you
must be of stone if you're not pierced too.

Deep in our souls let us be pierced,   23
and placate the wrath of God by tears.
The day of wrath, the ultimate day,
comes quickly; it's not far away.

Look, he who suffered out of pity   24
is coming back to judge us strictly;
yes, he's returning, but is forced
to threaten us now; he has no choice.

The world itself, aroused to anger,   25
will grievously avenge its Maker,
and eternally torment the guilty –
justly, it's true, and yet with cruelty.

26 Vos iudicis estis discipuli,
    in scriptura divina seduli,
    christiani lucerne populi,
    contemptores presentis seculi.

27 Vos non estis virgines fatue,
    vestre non sunt lampades vacue,
    vasa vestra manant assidue
    caritatis oleo mutue.

28 Vos pascitis gregem dominicum,
    erogantes divinum triticum,
    quibusdam plus, quidbusdam modicum,
    prout quemque scitis famelicum.

29 Decus estis ecclesiasticum;
    cum venerit iudex in publicum,
    ut puniat omne maleficum,
    sedebitis in thronis iudicum.

30 Verumtamen in mundi fluctibus,
    ubi nemo mundus a sordibus,
    que dicitis in vestris cordibus
    conpungendum est in cubilibus.

31 Insistite piis operibus,
    bene vestris utentes opibus;
    nam deo dat qui dat inopibus:
    ipse deus est in pauperibus.

32 Ut divina testatur pagina,
    opes multe sunt iusto sarcina;
    summa virtus est elemosina –
    dici debet virtutum domina.

33 Hanc conmendo vobis pre ceteris:
    abscondatur in sinu pauperis.
    Crede mihi, si quid deliqueris,
    per hanc deum placare poteris.

34 Hanc conmendo vobis precipue,
    hec est via vite perpetue,

30.3 *que* Wa. and Dr.; *quod* Ma.

You are the Judge's own disciples   26
and the lights of the Christian people,
eager to read the word of truth,
contemptuous of this life on earth.

You are not the foolish virgins;   27
your lamps aren't empty of their contents;
your vessels are flowing constantly
with the oil of mutual charity.

You are feeding the flock of the Lord,   28
sharing out the divine wheat-hoard –
more to one and less to another,
knowing the size of each man's hunger.

You are the glory of the Church.   29
When he comes openly, the Judge,
to bring each sinner to punishment,
you will be enthroned in judgement.

However, in the world's commotion   30
where no one's free from contamination,
you must repent what you have said
within your hearts, when you go to bed.

Take up good works, and use your wealth   31
charitably; for God himself
is in the poor; what you bestow
on them you're giving to God also.

In holy scripture it is written;   32
great wealth, to a just man, is a burden;
charity is the greatest of all
the virtues: their queen, it should be called.

Above all, this is my advice: 33
put something in the poor man's purse.
Believe me, if you've sinned or erred
this action will placate the Lord.

This in particular I commend;   34
this is the way of life without end,

quod salvator ostendens congrue
dixit: Omni petenti tribue.

35 Scitis ista, neque vos doceo;
sed quod scitis, facere moneo!
Pro me loqui iam tandem debeo –
non sum puer, etatem habeo.

36 Vitam meum vobis enucleo,
paupertatem meam non taceo:
sic sum pauper et sic indigeo,
quod tam siti quam fame pereo.

37 Non sum nequam, nullum decipio,
uno tantum laboro vitio:
nam libenter semper accipio
et plus mihi quam fratri cupio.

38 Si vendatur propter denarium
indumentum quod porto varium,
grande mihi fiet obprobrium –
malo diu pati ieiunium.

39 Largissimus largorum omnium
presul dedit hoc mihi pallium,
magis habens in celis premium
quam Martinus, qui dedit medium.

40 Nunc est opus ut vestra copia
sublevetur vatis inopia:
dent nobiles dona nobilia –
aurum, vestes, et his similia.

41 Ne pauperi sit excusacio:
det quadrantem gazofilacio;
hec vidue fuit oblacio,
quam divina conmendat racio.

42 Viri digni fama perpetua,
prece vestra complector genua:
ne recedam hinc manu vacua,
fiat pro me collecta mutua.

43 Mea vobis patet intencio;
vos gravari sermone sencio,

as our Saviour fittingly displayed:
'Give to everyone who asks' he said.

You know this – I'm not teaching you;   35
but what you know, I warn you to do!
Now I must speak at last for myself –
I'm not a boy, I have years enough.

I'll tell you my life-history,   36
and shan't conceal my poverty:
I'm so poor, in such desperation,
I'm dying of thirst and of starvation.

I'm not wicked or deceiving;   37
I've only one vice: I like receiving
whatever's given; and I'd rather
more came to me than to my brother.

If I had to sell, for the sake   38
of money, the grey and white fur cloak
I wear, it would bring me great dishonour –
I'd rather endure long days of hunger.

The most generous of all great-   39
hearted prelates gave me this coat,
thus earning more reward in heaven
than Martin, who gave half of one.

Now it's time for the prophet's poverty   40
to be relieved by your generosity:
let the nobles give noble presents –
clothing, gold, and suchlike objects.

Nor shall the poor be freed from giving   41
to the treasury their farthing:
that was the widow's contribution,
which earned a divine commendation.

Now I embrace your knees, while praying,   42
my lords, whose fame should be undying:
let mutual collecting be started
so that I don't leave empty-handed.

Having shown my intention clearly,   43
I feel that you are burdened sorely

unde finem sermonis facio,
quem sic finit brevis oracio:

44 Prestet vobis creator Eloy
caritatis lechitum olei,
spei vinum, frumentum fidei
et post mortem ad vitam provehi –

45 nobis vero mundo fruentibus
vinum bonum sepe bibentibus,
sine vino deficientibus,
nummos multos pro largis sumptibus.

                                    Amen.

II

Fama tuba dante sonum,
excitata vox preconum
clamat viris regionum,
advenire virum bonum,
5 patrem pacis et patronum,
cui Vienna parat tronum.
multitudo marchionum,
turba strepens istrionum
iam conformat tono tonum.
10 genus omne balatronum
intrat ante diem nonum:
quisque sperat grande donum.
ego caput fero pronum
tanquam frater sim latronum,
15 [r]eus, inops racionum,
sensus egens et sermonum.

Nomen vatis vel personam
manifeste non exponam,
sed, quem fuga fecit Ionam,
20 per figuram satis bonam
Ione nomen ei ponam.

Lacrimarum fluit rivus,
quas effundo fugitivus
intra cetum semivivus,

by what I preach; so I'll finish here,
and end my sermon with this brief prayer:

To you may the Creator, Eloy,   44
grant the cruse of the oil of charity,
the wine of hope, the corn of faith,
and conveyance to life after death.

To me, who often drink good wine,   45
who feel at death's door if there's none,
who so enjoy the world's delights,
may he grant huge funds for my vast debts.
                                        Amen.

II

Trumpets sound, and Fame announces,
as the heralds raise their voices
calling to the local masses,
that a man of worth approaches;
Vienne is waiting with a throne for   5
peace's father and defender.
There's a multitude of princes;
and a crowd of loud performers
harmonizing notes in chorus.
Every kind of fool and jester,   10
well before the date, came hither
hoping for a wealthy bonus.
I, though, hang my head and cower
like a man who's kin to robbers,
guilty, scarcely in my senses,   15
void of feelings, almost speechless.

What's the poet's name, his status?
I'm not going to unveil him;
but, since he ran off like Jonah,
that will serve him as an alias: 20
Jonah is what I shall call him.

All the floods of tears I've shed
made a river as I fled
here inside the whale, half-dead –

25 tuus quondam adoptivus.
sed pluralis genitivus,
nequam nimis et lascivus.
mihi factus est nocivus.

Voluptate volens frui
30 conparabar brute sui
nec cum sancto sanctus fui,
unde timens iram tui,
sicut Ionas dei sui,
fugam petens fuga rui.

35 Ionam deprehensum sorte,
reum tempestatis orte,
condempnatum a cohorte
mox absorbent ceti porte.
sic et ego dignus morte
40 prave vivens et distorte,
cuius carnes sunt absorte
(sed cor manet adhuc forte)
reus tibi vereor te,
miserturum mihi forte.

45 Ecce Ionas tuus plorat;
culpam suam non ignorat,
pro qua cetus eum vorat,
veniam vult et implorat,
ut a peste, qua laborat,
50 solvas eum, quem honorat
tremit colit et adorat.

Si remittas hunc reatum
et si ceto des mandatum,
cetus, cuius os est latum,
55 more suo dans hiatum
vomet vatem decalvatum
et ad portum destinatum
feret fame tenuatum,
ut sit rursus vates vatum
60 scribens opus tibi gratum.

---

41 *absorte* = CL *absorbtae.*
42-3 My punctuation follows Wa.

I, your son once, by adoption.   25
But my constant fornication,
wicked lust and dissipation,
quite destroyed my reputation.

Wallowing in pleasure grossly
I was like a pig, and beastly –   30
not a saint among the saintly.
Therefore, fearful of your fury,
just as Jonah feared the Almighty's,
I retreated in a hurry.

When the crew cast lots, the blame   35
for the rising of the storm
fell on Jonah; they condemned him
and the monster's jaws engulfed him.
Likewise I've deserved to die, by
living badly and corruptly,   40
so that I've worn out my body
(though my heart's still beating stoutly);
I'm afraid of you, and guilty,
but perhaps I'll gain your pity.

Look: your Jonah's weeping, conscious   45
of his lamentable weakness –
that for which the whale devoured him;
he implores you to forgive him:
save him from the doom that's crushed him –
he so honours you and fears you   50
and respectfully adores you.

If you will forgive this error
and give orders to the monster,
to the whale with its huge gullet,
it will stretch its jaws and vomit   55
from them your bald-headed poet –
now much thinner from starvation –
to his proper destination;
then he'll write again, as leading
poet, work you'll relish reading.   60

te divine mentis fatum
ad hoc iussit esse natum,
ut decore probitatum
et exemplis largitatum
65 reparares mundi statum.

Hunc reatum si remittas,
inter enses et sagittas
tutus ibo, quo me mittas,
hederarum ferens vittas.

70 Non timebo Ninivitas
[n]eque gentes infronitas;
[vin]cam vita patrum vitas,
vitans ea, que tu vitas.
poetrias inauditas
75 scribam tibi, si me ditas.

Ut iam loquar manifeste:
paupertatis premor peste
stultus ego, qui penes te
nummis equis victu veste
80 dies omnes duxi feste,
nunc insanus plus Oreste
male vivens et moleste
trutannizans inhoneste
omne festum duco meste;
85 res non eget ista teste.

Pacis auctor, ultor litis,
esto vati tuo mitis
neque credas imperitis!
genitivis iam sopitis
90 sanctior sum heremitis.
quicquid in me malum scitis,
amputabo, si velitis;
ne nos apprehendat sitis,
ero palmes et tu vitis.

From your birth you were ordained
by God's will to use your noble
powers of goodness and your liberal
generosity to amend
the condition of the world.   65
If you will forgive my frailty,
I'll go anywhere you send me –
walk through swords and arrows safely –
garlanded in wreaths of ivy.

Ninevites and suchlike people,   70
crude and bold, won't make me tremble;
I'll be saintlier than a hermit;
if you shun a thing, I'll shun it.
I'll write you poems the likes of which
aren't heard of, if you'll make me rich.   75

Let me make my meaning plain:
poverty's what weighs me down –
fool that I am; in your service
every day was spent in gladness –
food and clothing, money, horses.   80
Now I'm wilder than Orestes,
living dismally, and cadging
what I need by shameful begging;
every holiday's a sadness;
that's a thing that needs no witness.   85

Peacemaker and quarrel-settler,
sir, please treat your poet gently;
don't believe the stupid prattlers;
now my lusts are quelled completely,
and no hermit is so saintly.   90
Whatever's bad in me, just say:
for you it shall be pruned away.
So that I don't go short of wine,
I'll be the branch and you the vine.

III

Omnia tempus habent, et ego breve postulo tempu	s,
Ut possim paucos presens tibi reddere versu	s,
Electo sacro presens in tegmine macr	o.
Virgineo more non hec loquor absque rubor	e.
5 Vive, vir inmense, tibit concedit regimen s	e,
Consilio cuius regitur validaque manu iu	s.
Pontificum flos es et maximus inter eos e	s,
Incolumis vivas, plus Nestore consilii va	s.
Vir pie, vir iuste, precor, ut moneam precibus t	e,
10 Vir racione vigens, dat honorem tota tibi gen	s.
Amplecti minimos magni solet esse viri mo	s.
Cor miseris flecte, quoniam probitas docet hec t	e.
Pauperie plenos solita pietate fove no	s,
Et transmontanos, vir transmontane, iuva no	s.
15 Nulla mihi certe de vita spes nisi per t	e.
Frigore sive fame tolletur spiritus a m	e,
Asperitas brume necat horriferumque gelu m	e,
Continuam tussim pacior, tanquam tisicus si	m.
Sencio per pulsum, quod non a morte procul su	m.
20 Esse probant inopes nos corpore cum reliquo pe	s.
Unde verecundo vultu tibi verba precum d	o:
In tali veste non sto sine fronte penes t	e.
Liber ab interitu sis et memor esto mei t	u!

IV

1 Archicancellarie, vir discrete mentis,
   cuius cor non agitur levitatis ventis,
   aut morem transgreditur viri sapientis,
   non est in me forsitan id, quod de me sentis.

2 Audi preces, domine, veniam petentis,
   exaudi suspiria gemitusque flentis
   et opus inpositum ferre non valentis,
   quod probare potero multis argumentis.

III

To everything there is a season, and I ask a brief season
so that I may present these few verses to you in person,
I in a cloak that's threadbare,   and you, elected our high leader;
I say this like a maiden –   shyly, that is, and blushing crimson.
Hail, man of mighty power!   The state's entrusted to your care;   5
the law's at the command   of your good judgement and strong
    hand.
You are the priesthood's flower;   no other man of God stands
    higher.
Long life and health! You've more   wisdom than Nestor's in your
    store.
Just man, and man of virtue,   I pray that by my prayers I'll move
    you.
All people in this land   honour you, man of powerful mind.   10
A great man will embrace   those who are in the lowest place.
Have mercy on the plight   of beggars: such concern is right.
With your accustomed care   for duty, cherish us who are poor.
As a Tramontane, you   should help me; I'm Tramontane too.
I have no certain hope   of life unless I get your help.   15
Hunger and cold will steal   away from me my breath and soul.
The winter's bitter chill   and horrifying cold may kill;
I suffer as if I'm   consumptive, coughing all the time.
My pulse gives me a sense   that now my death is not far hence.
My body and, what's more,   my feet show that I'm really poor.   20
So I can't help but be   embarrassed as I make my plea –
I feel ashamed to come   before your eyes, dressed as I am.
I pray you'll be assigned   long life; and please keep me in mind.

IV

Wise archchancellor, well known for your discrimination,   1
on whose heart the winds of change don't make an impression,
you who never stray from your habit of discretion:
I may not be able to meet your expectation.

Master, listen to my prayers as I beg for mercy;   2
hear the sighs and groans of one shedding tears of misery
and unable to sustain the burden that he's under:
I can prove it, having much evidence to offer.

3 Tuus in perpetuum servus et poeta
  ibo, si preceperis, eciam trans freta,
  et quodcumque iusseris, scribam mente leta,
  sed angusti temporis me coartat meta.

4 Iubes angustissimo spacio dierum
  me tractare seriem augustarum rerum,
  quas neque Virgilium posse nec Homerum
  annis quinque scribere constat esse verum.

5 Vis et infra circulum parve septimane
  bella scribam forcia breviter et nane,
  que vix in quinquennio scriberes, Lucane,
  vel tu, vatum maxime, Maro Mantuane.

6 Vir virorum optime, parce tuo vati,
  qui se totum subicit tue voluntati.
  precor, cum non audeam opus tantum pati,
  ut rigorem temperes ardui mandati.

7 Nosti, quod in homine non sit eius via:
  prophecie spiritus fugit ab Helya,
  Helyseum deserit sepe prophetia,
  nec me [semper] sequitur mea poetria.

8 Aliquando facio versus mille cito,
  et tunc nulli cederem versuum perito;
  sed post tempus modicum, cerebro sopito,
  versus a me fugiunt carminis oblito.

9 Que semel emittitur, nescit vox reverti,
  scripta sua corrigunt eciam diserti;
  [ver]sus volunt corrigi denuoque verti,
  [ne] risum segnicies pariat inerti.

10 Loca vitant publica quidam poetarum
   et secretas eligunt sedes latebrarum,
   student instant vigilant nec laborant parum,
   et vix tandem reddere possunt opus clarum.

11 Jeiunant et abstinent poetarum chori,
   vitant rixas publicas et tumultus fori,

5,2 *nane*: an adverb derived irregularly from *nanus* – 'dwarfishly'. The word does not occur in lexica. Ma. suggests (ineptly) that *plane* may have been intended.

6,1 Wa. prints *vivorum*, without comment: a printing error, perhaps, or a misreading.

As your servant and your poet – yours for ever – I   3
will, if you should so command, even cross the sea,
and whatever works you may order I'll write gladly;
but the deadline, being so close, constrains me sadly.

You command that by a time just a few days hence   4
I should treat a series of notable events
which, it is a well known fact, Vergil or yet Homer
even in the space of five years would fail to cover.

You desire that in the space of a week, no more,   5
I write a brief and dwarfish account of valiant wars –
such a thing as scarcely in five years could be written
by the greatest poet, Mantuan Vergil, or by Lucan.

So, most excellent of men, spare your poet, who   6
totally submits to what you may bid him do.
I beseech you, since I don't dare to bear this burden,
please relax the stringency of your harsh injunction.

As you know, the way of man's not in his own keeping;   7
thus Elijah lost the spirit of prophetic speaking;
likewise, often, prophecy would desert Elisha;
neither do my poems come always at my pleasure.

There are times when I compose a thousand verses quickly;   8
then I yield to no one who's skilled in writing poetry;
but before much time has gone by my brain is flagging:
verses flee from me, and I forget the art of singing.

Words can never be called back, once they have been spoken;   9
even men of eloquence revise what they have written;
verses must be made anew and undergo revision,
or his laziness may bring the amateur derision.

Certain poets tend to shun places that are public   10
and secrete themselves away somewhere claustrophobic;
sleeplessly they toil and strive; yet, for all their grinding,
seldom manage to produce anything outstanding.

Fasting and teetotal, these choirs of singing poets   11
keep away from public strife and the market's tumults;

et ut opus faciant, quod non possit mori,
moriuntur studio subditi labori.

12 Unicuique proprium dat natura munus:
ego nunquam potui scribere ieiunus;
me ieiunum vincere posset puer unus,
sitim et ieiunium odi quasi funus.

13 Unicuique proprium dat natura donum:
ego versus faciens bibo vinum bonum,
et quod habent melius dolia cauponum,
tale vinum generat copiam sermonum.

14 Tales versus facio, quale vinum bibo,
nichil possum facere nisi sumpto cibo;
nichil valent penitus, que ieiunus scribo,
Nasonem post calices carmine preibo.

15 Michi nunquam spiritus prophetie datur,
nisi prius fuerit venter bene satur;
dum in arce cerebri Bachus dominatur,
in me Phebus irruit et miranda fatur.

16 Scribere non valeo pauper et mendicus,
que gessit in Latio Cesar Fredericus,
qualiter subactus est Tuscus inimicus,
preter te, qui Cesaris integer amicus.

17 Poeta pauperior omnibus poetis,
nichil prorsus habeo, nisi quod videtis.
unde sepe lugeo, quando vos ridetis;
nec me meo vitio pauperem putetis.

18 Fodere non debeo, quia sum scolaris,
ortus ex militibus preliandi gnaris;
sed quia me terruit labor militaris,
malui Virgilium sequi quam te, Paris.

19 Mendicare pudor est, mendicare nolo,
fures multa possident, sed non absque dolo.
quid ergo iam faciam, qui nec agros colo,
nec mendicus fieri nec fur esse volo?

20 Sepe de miseria mee paupertatis
conqueror in carmine viris litteratis;

in their efforts to compose works which live for ever
they expire in the attempt out of sheer endeavour.

Nature has made each of us idiosyncratic: 12
I could never write a word with an empty stomach;
any child could knock me down when I haven't eaten;
thirst and hunger are to me hateful as extinction.

Each of us, by nature, is given some advantage.   13
When I'm writing verse I drink wine of decent vintage
and the best that's to be found in the landlord's pantry;
wine like that will generate rhetoric in plenty.

How I write is governed by the kind of wine I swallow;   14
poetry's impossible when my stomach's hollow;
what I write when fasting is feeble and insipid;
when I've had a glass or two I can outsing Ovid.

I am never given prophetic inspiration   15
if my stomach isn't first sated to repletion;
but when Bacchus holds his sway in my mental fortress,
Phoebus rushes into me and pronounces wonders.

I shall not be fit to portray, poor and a beggar,   16
the campaigns in Italy of Frederick, our Caesar,
how he crushed the Tuscan foe; I can go no further
than to write of you, who are the loyal friend of Caesar.

As a poet poorer than all the poets, I   17
don't own anything at all apart from what you see;
which is why I'm often lamenting when you're laughing;
you should not imagine I'm poor through my own doing.

Digging isn't right for me, because I am a scholar,   18
born of knightly family, skilled in arts of warfare;
but because I had no heart for military labour
I chose Vergil rather than Paris as my mentor.

Begging is a shameful thing, I will not go begging;   19
thieves possess a lot, but they get it by deceiving.
Therefore what am I to do, with no fields to till,
and no willingness to go begging or to steal?

Often I complain in my verse, to men of learning,   20
of the great distress that my poverty is causing;

laici non capiunt ea, que sunt vatis,
et nil mi retribuunt, quod est notum satis.

21 A viris Teutonicis multa solent dari,
digni sunt pre ceteris laude singulari.

. . . .
. . . .

22 Presules Italie presules avari,
pocius ydolatre debent nominari:
vix quadrantem tribuunt pauperi scolari.
quis per dona talia poterit ditari?

23 Doleo, cum video leccatores multos
penitus inutiles penitusque stultos,
nulla prorsus animi racione fultos
sericis et variis indumentis cultos.

24 Vellem, soli milites eis ista darent,
et de nobis presules nostri cogitarent;
non leonum spoliis asinos ornarent,
sed dum querent gloriam, pietate carent.

25 Eia nunc pontifices pietatis mire,
cum poeta soleat foris esurire,
mimi solent cameras vestras introire,
qui nil sciunt facere preter insanire.

26 Pereat ypocrisis omnium parcorum,
scimus quod avarus est cultor ydolorum.
commendetur largitas presulum largorum:
electus Colonie primus est eorum.

27 In regni negociis potens et peritus
a regni negocio nomen est sortitus,
precepti dominici memor, non oblitus
tribuit hilariter, non velud invitus.

28 Inde fit, ut aliquid petere presumam:
nudus ego, metuens frigus atque brumam,
qui vellus non habeo nec in lecto plumam,
tam libenter mihi det, quam libenter sumam.

21.22 These six lines are linked by the same rhyme. Grimm joined them together as one
strophe. Ma., following Schmeidler, separates them as above, assuming a gap in the text.

laymen just don't know the situation of a poet,
and (the fact's quite evident) they give me nothing for it.

Plenty's given by the men of the German race: 21
they, above all others, deserve unusual praise.

The Italian bishops, though, are as mean as misers;   22
rather they deserve the name of idolaters;
for the most they give a poor scholar is a farthing:
who could ever be made rich by so small an offering?

I'm unhappy when I see the many parasites,   23
all completely useless and completely without wits,
totally devoid of any intellectual power,
all dressed up in silks and coats of variegated fur.

What I wish is that the knights, and only they, would be   24
generous to them, while our bishops thought of me,
rather than use lions' skins to make asses look pretty;
but in their quest for glory they are lacking in all pity.

Look at you now, priests with your wonderful compassion: 25
while the poet stays outside, suffering starvation,
clowns habitually go into your apartments,
who have no accomplishments other than their nonsense.

Woe to the hypocrisy of the niggardly!   26
As we know, the miser's cult is idolatry.
Let the bounty of free-giving bishops be commended;
first among them is the one whom Cologne's elected.

In the kingdom's business he's a powerful man, and skilled: 27
from a "regal" source he got his name of "Reginald";
mindful, not forgetful, of God our Master's teaching,
he gives cheerfully, and not as if he were unwilling.

So it is that I presume to utter a request: 28
being short of clothes, I fear winter's cold and frost;
I've no fleece, no down upon my bed; so let him give
willingly, and I'd be just as willing to receive.

29 Archicancellarie, spes es mea solus,
    in te non est macula, non est in te dolus.
    longa tibi tempora det fatalis colus,
    cuius illustrabitur claritate polus.

30 Nummos, quos tu dederas, bene dispensavi:
    pauperem presbiterum hac estate pavi,
    ut te deus protegat in labore gravi
    et coram te corruant inimici pravi.

31 Largum habens dominum nolo parcus esse,
    nolo sine socio mea frui messe;
    nobilis est animi, pluribus prodesse,
    largo nunquam poterit animo deesse.

32 Secundum quod habeo, tribuo libenter,
    neque panem comedo solus et latenter,
    et non sum, qui curias intrem imprudenter,
    sicut illi faciunt, quorum deus venter.

33 Archicancellarie, spes et vita mea,
    in quo mens est Nestoris et vox Ulixea,
    Christus tibi tribuat annos et trophea
    et nobis facundiam, ut scribamus ea.

V

1 Nocte quadam sabbati somno iam refectus,
   cum mihi fastidio factus esset lectus,
   signo crucis muniens frontem vultum pectus
   indui me vestibus, quibus eram tectus.

2 Sic dum nec accumberem neque starem rectus,
   tantus odor naribus meis est iniectus,
   quantum numquam protulit spica nardi nec thus
   neque liquor balsami recens et electus.

3 Ortus erat lucifer, stella matutina,
   cum perfusus undique luce repentina
   sum raptus ad ethera quadam vi divina;
   ubi deus raptor est, dulcis est rapina.

4 Repente sub pedibus hunc relinquo mundum
   et in orbem videor ingredi secundum,

You, archchancellor, are my hope, and you alone;   29
there is no deceit in you, in you there is no stain.
May fate's spinning distaff grant you a long span;
then, made brilliant by your clear light, the sky will shine.

The money you had given I have honourably used: 30
in the summer I made payments to a hard-up priest,
so that God might guard you in your difficult exertions
and your wicked enemies collapse before your presence.

As my master's generous I don't want to be mean;   31
I'm reluctant to enjoy my harvest on my own,
for a noble spirit will be benevolent;
never will a generous spirit be in want.

In accordance with what I possess, I willingly   32
give, and I don't eat my bread alone and secretly;
nor do I go into great houses without heed,
as do those for whom their own stomach is their god.

You, archchancellor, are my hope and my existence,   33
having Nestor's intellect and speaking like Ulysses;
so may Christ bestow on you triumphs and long years,
and on me the eloquence to put them into verse.

V

Once I woke before the dawn on a Sunday morning   1
when I'd slept enough, and to lie in bed was boring;
with the cross I blessed myself – forehead, face and breast –
took the clothes I'd slept beneath, and was getting dressed.

While I thus was in between lying down and standing,   2
such a scent assailed my nose it was quite astounding:
nothing like it ever rose up from nard or incense;
nor could finest balsam-oil give out such an essence.

Lucifer, the morning star, had already risen   3
when I was surrounded by light, profuse and sudden,
and a supernatural force carried me to heaven;
when it's God who snatches you, that's a sweet abduction.

Suddenly I seemed to leave this world altogether,   4
down below my feet, and go into quite another;

cuius admirabile lumen et iocundum
non valet exprimere verbis os facundum.

5 Non est ibi gemitus neque vox dolentis,
ubi sanctus populus inmortalis gentis
liber a periculis, tutus a tormentis
pace summa fruitur et quiete mentis.

6 [I]bi pulchritudinem vidi domus dei,
ipsum tamen oculi non videre mei,
nam divine tantus est splendor faciei,
quod mirantur angeli, qui ministrant ei.

7 Hic nec Aristotilem vidi nec Homerum,
tamen de sentenciis nominum et rerum,
de naturis generum atque specierum
magnus mihi protulit Augustinus verum.

8 Post hec ad archangelum loquens Michaelem,
qui regit per angelos populum fidelem,
ab eo sum monitus, ut secreta celem
et celi consilia nemini revelem.

9 Unde quamvis cernerem de futuris multa,
que sunt intellectibus hominum sepulta,
celi tamen prodere vereor occulta.
tu vero ne timeas, presul, sed exulta.

10 Tibi deputatus est unus angelorum,
super omnes alios os habens decorum,
sicut tu virtutibus operum clarorum
meritis preradias omnium proborum.

11 Huius ope prelia tu vicisse scias,
ut des deo gloriam, nec superbus fias,
tui dux itineris est per omnes vias,
pro tuis excessibus preces fundens pias.

12 Per hunc regnum Siculum fiet tui iuris,
ad radicem arboris ponitur securis:
tyrannus extollitur et est sine curis,
sed eius interitus venit instar furis.

---

[9],3 *vereor* Wa., following Meyer. Ma. has *videor*, but this makes less good sense with
tamen.

what amazing light it had, what delightful radiance,
the most eloquent of mouths couldn't tell in language.

There no grieving voice is heard, nor the sound of weeping,   5
where the holy tribe of the immortals in God's keeping,
free from any danger and safe from any torment,
lives in perfect peace of mind and serene contentment.

There I saw the glorious beauty of God's mansion,   6
but the Lord himself did not come into my vision;
for his holy countenance is so bright and splendid
that the very angels who serve him are confounded.

Aristotle wasn't there, nor did I see Homer;   7
but the great St Augustine gave me truth to ponder,
teaching me the nature of genera and species
and the differences between objects and ideas.

After this I had some talk with the Archangel Michael,   8
who with all his angel host rules the faithful people;
he gave warning that I must keep their secrets hidden
and reveal to nobody what is planned in heaven.

So although I learned a good deal about the future –   9
things that human minds are not shown, such is our nature –
I shall keep the secrets of heaven, being fearful.
You, though, Bishop, need not fear: no, you should be joyful.

You have been allotted one angel, of such beauty   10
that he far surpasses all others in his glory,
just as you outshine by your virtues and your noble
actions all the merits of other upright people.

By his aid your enemies came to be defeated;   11
knowing this, you should thank God and not be conceited;
on your every journey you have this angel's guidance;
also he devotedly prays for your transgressions.

Through him Sicily shall be yours to oversee,   12
for the axe is at the root, threatening the tree;
now the tyrant flaunts his power with no care or grief,
but his ruin's on its way, silent as a thief.

13 Nolo tibi denique nimium blandiri,
    neque meo domino blandiens mentiri;
    nemo potest adeo mundus inveniri,
    ut sit sine macula mens et actus viri.

14 Ille sanctus inclitus, gemma sacerdotum,
    cuius nomen omnibus reor esse notum,
    qui suis miraculis replet orbem totum,
    se dicit adversum te nimis esse motum.

15 Cumque vellet conqueri de te coram deo,
    vix querelam distulit flexus fletu meo;
    flebam namque graviter, sicut sepe fleo,
    lacrimis inducias postulans ab eo.

16 Fluebant ab oculis lacrimarum rivi,
    et quia conpescere lacrimas nequivi,
    de terra ridencium lacrimans exivi,
    inventus in lectulo more semivivi.

17 Precor ergo: domine, flos presentis evi,
    ut ad sancti gratiam redeas in brevi,
    res eius diripiunt quidam lupi sevi,
    quas tu restituere verbo potes levi.

18 Quamvis incessabilis sarcina curarum
    mentem tuam distrahat nec fatiget parum,
    scire tamen opus est, quod sit deo carum,
    iuvare viriliter res ecclesiarum.

19 Fac ergo concordiam sancto cum Martino,
    qui pro te multociens me potavit vino;
    quod hec pax sit melior quam cum Palatino,
    novit quisquis agitur spiritu divino.

20 Cum te vir sanctissimus vellet accusare,
    vix eum prohibui lacrimans amare;
    et quia sic volui pro te laborare,
    debes mihi magnum quid in hoc festo dare.

21 Tussis indeficiens et defectus vocis
    cum ruinam nuncient obitus velocis,

19.2 *multociens* = CL *multoties.*

I shan't overpraise you, my master; I'm not willing   13
to extend my flattery to the point of lying.
No one in the world can be found who's so untarnished
that his actions and his mind are without a blemish.

There's a certain famous saint, jewel of the priesthood,   14
known by name to all, I feel sure, and celebrated,
who has spread his miracles through the world in plenty;
he declares that you, my lord, make him very angry.

When he wanted to denounce you to God, I swayed him   15
by my bitter weeping, which just in time delayed him;
for I sorely wept (as I do – my weeping's frequent),
and with tears I begged him to grant you a postponement.

Tears were pouring from my eyes – rivers of them, streaming –   16
and because there was no way I could stop my weeping
I went out in tears from that country of the laughing,
and I found myself in bed, only just surviving.

Therefore, sir, I beg of you, flower of our era,   17
do make haste to please the saint and regain his favour;
savage wolves are robbing him, seizing his possessions,
which you could restore to him with a casual sentence.

Greatly though you're burdened by weighty cares of office   18
which distract and weary you, seeming to be endless,
all the same you ought to know what the Lord would welcome:
vigorous support for church interests would please him.

Therefore make a treaty of peace now with St Martin,   19
who on your behalf has served wine to me so often;
such a treaty anyone moved by the divine
spirit would prefer to one with the Palatine.

When that holiest of men wanted to accuse you   20
I wept bitterly, and just managed to excuse you;
so, because on your behalf I made such an effort,
you should on this festal day give me a large present.

Now the failure of my voice and my constant coughing   21
prophesy my doom: a swift death is in the offing;

circumdant me gemitus in secretis locis,
nec iam libet solitis delectari iocis.

22 Quamvis tamen moriar et propinquem fini,
et me fata terreant obitus vicini,
non possum diligere nomen Palatini,
per quem facta carior est lagena vini;

23 Afflixit iniuriis populum et clerum.
sed de tot iniuriis diversarum rerum
ego non conquererer, ut iam loquar verum,
nisi michi carius venderetur merum.

24 Ut tyrannis comitis exponatur ipsi,
tales versus facio, quales nunquam scripsi:
omne ve, quod scribitur in Apocalipsi,
ferat, nisi liberet vites ab eclipsi.

25 Interim me dominus iuxta psalmum David
regit et in pascue claustro collocavit.
hic michi, non aliis, vinum habundavit;
abbas bonus pastor est et me bene pavit.

VI

En habeo versus, te precipiente, reversus,
sit [tibi] frons leta, versus recitante poeta:
laudibus eternum nullus negat esse Salernum;
illuc pro morbis totus circumfluit orbis,
5 nec debet sperni, fateor, doctrina Salerni,
quamvis exosa mihi sit gens illa dolosa,
quid sim passus ibi, nequit ex toto modo scribi:
iam febre vexatus nimioque dolore gravatus
hic infirmabar, quod vivere posse negabar,
10 et michi dicebant medici, qui signa videbant:
ecce, poeta, peris, non vives, sed morieris!
sed febrem tandem medicina fugavit eandem.
nostri languoris testis tibi sit color oris:
in vultu pallor apparet adhuc, nisi fallor.
15 dum sapiens fieri cupio medicusque videri,
insipiens factus sum mendicare coactus.
nunc mendicorum socius sum, non medicorum,
nudus et incultus cunctis appareo stultus.
pro vili panno sum vilis parque trutanno.

I'm accompanied by sighs in my lonely corner,
and my usual pastimes no longer give me pleasure.

Yet although I'm dying fast and my life is ending 22
and I'm terrified of my death which is impending,
still there's no way I can love that Count Palatine
who has caused the rise in price of a flask of wine.

He has done great harm to the clergy and the laity, 23
but the damage that he's done, in its great variety,
I should not complain about, I may say sincerely,
if the wine I buy were not costing me more dearly.

So to make the Count aware of his own oppression, 24
I'll write verse the likes of which I have never written:
may each kind of woe described in the Apocalypse
strike him if he won't release wine from this eclipse.

Meanwhile as in David's psalm the Lord is my master 25
and has given me a place in a cloistered pasture;
others may be short of wine: my cup runneth over;
thanks to my good shepherd – the abbot – I'm in clover.

VI

As you advised, I've come   back; and look, I have a poem.
May pleasure light your face, as   the poet reads aloud his verses.
Salerno, none denies,   is worthy of eternal praise –
a town to which the world   flocks with diseases to be cured;
the learning in that place   deserves all credit, I confess, 5
much as I find hateful   the people there, who are deceitful.
Mere writing can't declare   in full the things I suffered there:
tormented and weighed down   by fever and excessive pain
I grew so weak and ill,   they thought I couldn't live at all;
the doctors who could see   my signs and symptoms said to me: 10
'Look how you waste away,   poet; you won't survive, you'll die.'
But in the end that fever   was cured by medicine; it's over.
The colour of my face   may testify how ill I was:
unless I'm much mistaken,   I've still a very pale complexion.
I wanted to grow wise   and be a doctor in men's eyes; 15
but I became instead   a fool, who's forced to beg for bread.
Now I mix with beggars   for company, and not with doctors;
scruffy and half-naked,   I strike everyone as stupid.
These rags make me appear   a common tramp and nothing more.

20 nec me nudavit ludus neque fur spoliavit,
   pro solo victu sic sum spoliatus amictu,
   pro victu vestes consumpsi, dii mihi testes!

   Dum redeo, didici populi tocius ab ore,
   quod tua distribuas solo pietatis amore;
25 per mundum redoles tanto bonitatis odore,
   Cesaris adiutor speciali dignus honore.

   Te pauper sequitur, te predicat omnis egenus,
   idcirco quod sis hilaris dator atque serenus;
   tu miseris pater es multa dulcedine plenus;
30 nulla quidem virtus est, a qua sis alienus.

   Cum de presulibus male quisque loquatur avaris,
   omnes extollunt te laudibus undique claris.
   tu cum trans Alpes famosus ut hic habearis,
   re famam superas, non a fama superaris.

35 Optime vir, cuius soror est et amica Minerva,
   qua bene cuncta regis quamvis in gente proterva,
   sic da pauperibus, sic in celis coacerva,
   ne totum dones aliis, vero michi serva.

   Vir pie, qui nunquam bursam pro paupere nodas,
40 quantum sis largus, largo michi munere prodas.
   inde poeta tuus scribam tibi carmen et odas.
   sit finis verbi verbum laudabile do, das.

VII

   Archicancellarie, viris maior ceteris,
   splendore prudentie, qua prudentes preteris,
3 [i]ubar es ecclesie, sicut sol est etheris.

   [Lau]des tibi canimus, cuius luce iubaris
   illustratur animus Friderici Cesaris;
6 quod libenter facimus, cum sis dator hilaris.

   Pollens bonis moribus et nitore generis
   in humanis artibus et divinis litteris
9 ter sis maior omnibus, nullo minor crederis.

---

9 *ter* Ma. (as in Go.); Wa. *cum* (as in Br.)

It wasn't gambling or   a thief that stripped me almost bare: 20
simply to get food   my clothing had to be removed;
I sold my clothes to buy   food, the gods will testify.

When I came back, I heard the people saying constantly
that you share out your goods from simple love of piety;
throughout the world is wafted your generosity's good odour –   25
the Emperor's right hand man, deserving special honour.

You're followed by the poor, and highly praised by all the needy,
because you are a cheerful giver, doing it so gladly;
you're a father to the wretched, filled with kindness in great measure;
indeed there is no virtue to which you are a stranger.   30

There may be nasty talk about bishops who are greedy,
but everyone in every quarter praises you most highly.
Your fame extends across the Alps, on either side the same,
but can't outshine the facts; you are superior to your fame.

Excellent sir, Minerva is your sister and your friend;   35
unruly though your people are, you rule with expert hand.
Give to the poor, and lay up treasure in heaven in such a way
that some of it is kept for me: don't give it all away.

Benevolent man, you never keep your purse closed to the poor;
give me a generous gift to match the generous man you are.   40
Then your poet will write the songs and verses you deserve.
Now let my speech end with the noble verb 'I give, you give'.

VII

You, Archchancellor, surpass other men in moral size;
with your wisdom you outshine brightly others who are wise;
you're the glory of the Church, as the sun is of the skies.   3

Singing praises we extol you, sir, who illuminate
with your brilliant light the mind of Frederick, who rules our state;
this we gladly do, since you give with such a cheerful heart.   6

Mighty through your noble birth and your own morality,
learned in both secular arts and in divinity,
thrice supreme: no other can claim superiority.   9

Vir fortis et sapiens fortunam non sequeris
in adversis paciens, modestus in prosperis,
12 cuncta bene faciens recta via graderis.

Ulixe facundior Tulliane loqueris,
columba simplicior nulli fraudes ingeris,
15 serpente callidior a nullo deciperis.

Alexandro forcior inimicos conteris,
David mansuetior a cunctis diligeris,
18 [et] Martino largior das, quod iuste peteris.

In regni negocio fit, quodcumque precipis,
qui sine consilio nichil prorsus incipis;
21 viget tanto socio mens Romani principis.

Adhuc starent menia Mediolanensium,
nec Cesar per prelia victor esset hostium,
24 nisi dei gracia te dedisset socium.

Electum Colonie claris dignum laudibus
pre multa pauperie nudis laudo pedibus,
27 conqueror hoc hodie coram sanctis omnibus.

Dum sanctorum omnium colitur celebritas,
singuli colentium gerunt vestes inclitas,
30 archicancellarii vatem pulsat nuditas.

Poeta composuit racionem rithmicam,
at Yrus imposuit melodiam musicam,
33 unde bene meruit mantellum et tunicam.

VIII

Presul urbis Agripine
qui rigorem discipline
    bonitate temperas,
nichil agens indiscrete,
ne sit fama mendax de te
    vita famam superas.

---

[21] *viget* Ma. 1929; in 1916 he had *invidet* (as in Go.)
[30] *archicancellarii vatem pulsat* Ma. (as in Go.) *archicancellarium vatis pulset* Wa.
[32] *at Yrus* Ma.

Wise and noble, you ignore Fortune in her fickle play;
patient in adversity, moderate in prosperous days,
doing all things well, you walk your undeviating way.   12

Smoother than Ulysses, your speech is Ciceronian;
you're more harmless than a dove, never cheating anyone,
yet, more cunning than a snake, you are never taken in.   15

Alexander never crushed enemies with stronger zeal;
David never was so kind (hence the love your people feel);
Martin was less generous: you grant any just appeal.   18

In the kingdom's government all that you advise is done,
since without considered thought you let nothing be begun;
and the Emperor's mind is strong, aided by so great a man.   21

To this day the city walls of the Milanese would stand:
Frederick would not have won martial victories in command,
if the grace of God had not sent you to assist his hand.   24

You deserve the highest praise, bishop chosen for Cologne;
but I praise you with bare feet: poverty has brought me down;
in the sight of all the saints on this day I make my moan.   27

When the festival of All Saints is celebrated here,
all the celebrating crowd dress in their most splendid gear,
but your poet, to his grief, won't have anything to wear.   30

I composed this rhythmical text – a poet's handiwork –
and the beggar has imposed tune and music on the work;
therefore I have rightly earned both a tunic and a cloak.   33

VIII

Lord of Agrippina's city,
kindness tempers the severity
    of your rule, and gives relief.
All you do's done with discretion;
you outdo your reputation
    (lest it should be false) by your life.

IX

1 Salve mundi domine, Cesar noster, ave,
   cuius bonis omnibus iugum est suave;
   quiquis contra calcitrat putans illud grave,
   obstinati cordis est et cervicis prave.

2 Princeps terre principum, Cesar Friderice,
   cuius tuba titubant arces inimice,
   tibi colla subdimus tygres et formice
   et cum cedris Libani vepres et mirice.

3 Nemo prudens ambigit, te per dei nutum
   super reges alios regem constitutum
   et in dei populo digne consecutum
   tam vindicte gladium quam tutele scutum.

4 Unde diu cogitans, quod non esset tutum,
   Cesari non reddere censum vel tributum,
   vidua pauperior tibi do minutum,
   de cuius me laudibus pudet esse mutum.

5 Tu foves et protegis magnos et minores,
   magnis et minoribus tue patent fores.
   Omnes ergo Cesari sumus debitores,
   qui pro nostra requie sustinet labores.

6 Dent fruges agricole, pisces piscatores,
   auceps volatilia, feras venatores:
   nos poete pauperes, opum contemptores,
   scribendo Cesareos canimus honores.

7 Filius ecclesie fidem sequor sanam,
   contempno gentilium falsitatem vanam,
   unde iam non invoco Febum vel Dianam
   nec a Musis postulo linguam Tullianam.

8 Christi sensus imbuat mentem Christianam,
   ut de Christo domino digna laude canam,
   qui potenter sustinens sarcinam mundanam
   relevat in pristinum gradum rem Romanam.

8.2 *domino* Ma. 1929; in 1916 he had *domini*, as does Wa.

IX

Hail the master of the world, greetings to our Caesar!   1
All the good and virtuous find your yoke is easy;
he who kicks against it, though, thinking it oppressive,
is a stiff-necked man, and his heart is unsubmissive.

Prince of princes of the earth, Frederick our Caesar,   2
at whose trumpet citadels of the enemy totter,
we bow down to you: the ants bow down, as do the tigers,
cedars from the Lebanon with humble shrubs and briars.

No one in his senses doubts that the will of God   3
set you up as king above all others by His nod
and that for God's people you honourably wield
both the sword of vengeance and the protecting shield.

For a long time I have thought it was risking danger   4
not to render tax and due tribute unto Caesar;
poorer than a widow I am, but here's my mite,
since in praise of you I'd feel ashamed of staying mute.

Great and humble share in your kindness and protection;   5
to both great and humble your doors are always open;
therefore we are, all of us, in the debt of Caesar,
who, to give us peaceful lives, undertakes such labour.

Let the fishermen give fish, let the farmers come   6
with their crops, the fowler give birds, the huntsmen game:
but we poets who are poor, scorning rich resources,
sing in Caesar's honour by writing him our verses.

I'm a son of mother Church, I follow the true faith;   7
I despise the heathen people's vain untruth;
therefore I do not invoke Diana or Apollo,
or entreat the Muses for the tongue of Cicero.

May the consciousness of Christ fill a Christian's mind   8
that I may sing in worthy praise of our anointed lord,
who supports the burden of the world with all his power,
raising up the Roman state to what it was before.

9 Scimus per desidiam regum Romanorum
   ortas in imperio spinas impiorum,
   et sumpsisse cornua multos populorum,
   de quibus commemoro gentem Lombardorum.

10 Que dum turres erigit more Giganteo,
   volens altis turribus obviare deo,
   contumax et fulmine digna Ciclopeo
   instituta principum sprevit ausu reo.

11 Libertatis titulo volens gloriari,
   nolens in Italia regem nominari,
   indignata regulis legum cohartari
   extra legum terminos cepit evagari.

12 De tributo Cesaris nemo cogitabat,
   omnes erant Cesares, nemo censum dabat;
   civitas Ambrosii velud Troia stabat,
   deos parum, homines minus formidabat.

13 Dives bonis omnibus et beata satis,
   nisi quia voluit repugnare fatis;
   cuius esse debuit summa libertatis,
   ut, quod erat Cesaris, daret ei gratis.

14 Surrexit interea rex, iubente deo,
   metuendus hostibus tamquam ferus leo,
   similis in preliis Jude Machabeo,
   de quo quicquid loquerer, minus esset eo.

15 Non est eius animus in curanda cute,
   curam carnis comprimit animi virtute;
   de communi cogitans populi salute,
   pravorum superbiam premit servitute.

16 Quanta sit potencia vel laus Friderici,
   cum sit patens omnibus, non est opus dici.
   qui rebelles lancea fodiens ultrici
   representat Karolum dextera victrici.

---

[11] This str. occurs only in Po, a 15th c. MS written in Cracow. Dronke sees it as a 'poorer version of str. 12' (see 'The Archpoet and the Classics', note 24). As he points out, if it were excised it would leave 33 strophes, bearing out the Archpoet's predilection for the 'perfect' numbers 33 and 100; poem IV has 33 strophes, VII 33 lines, V and X 100 lines.

When the Roman emperors were in decline, we know   9
that in the kingdom of the godless thorns began to grow,
and that many of the tribes entered on rebellion –
of which the Lombard people is the one I'll mention.

While this tribe erected towers in a giant mode,   10
wanting to go up in high towers to meet God,
in their arrogance they scorned imperial laws, deserving
a Cyclopean thunderbolt for their wicked daring.

Through their wish to glory in the name of liberty,   11
they refused to recognise a king in Italy;
angry at restriction by the laws which hedged them round,
they began to deviate beyond the legal bounds.

As for Caesar's tribute-money, no one thought about it: 12
all of them were Caesars now, no one paid the tribute;
the city of St Ambrose became as Troy had been,
having little fear of gods, and even less of men.

It was rich in everything, a happy enough state,   13
if it hadn't wanted to rebel against the fates;
the summit of its liberty ought to have been this:
willingly to offer to Caesar what was his.

Meanwhile, as commanded by God, the emperor rose   14
terrifying as a fierce lion to his foes,
similar in battle to Judas Maccabaeus;
anything I said of him would be less than he is.

What he has in mind is not caring for his skin: 15
mental valour overcomes bodily concern;
thinking always of the well-being of his people,
he crushes into servitude the hubris of the evil.

There's no need to say how great is Frederick's renown   16
or his might, since they are quite clear to everyone;
as he wounds the rebels with his avenging spear
he looks just like Charlemagne in his triumphant power.

17 Hic ergo considerans orbem conturbatum
    potenter agreditur opus deo gratum,
    et ut regnum revocet ad priorem statum,
    repetit ex debito census civitatum.

18 Prima suo domino paruit Papia,
    urbs bona, flos urbium, clara potens pia;
    digna foret laudibus et topographia,
    nisi quod nunc utimur brevitatis via.

19 Post Papiam ponitur urbs Novariensis,
    cuius pro imperio dimicavit ensis,
    frangens et reverberans viribus inmensis
    impetum superbie Mediolanensis.

20 Carmine, Novaria, semper meo vives,
    cuius sunt per omnia commendandi cives;
    inter urbes alias eris laude dives,
    donec desint Alpibus frigora vel nives.

21 Letare, Novaria, numquam vetus fies,
    meis tu carminibus renovari scies;
    fame tue terminus nullus erit dies,
    nunc est tibi reddita post laborem quies.

22 Mediolanensium dolor est inmensus,
    pre dolore nimio conturbatur sensus;
    civibus Ambrosii furor est accensus,
    dum ab eis petitur, ut a servis, census.

23 Interim precipio tibi, Constantine,
    Jam depone dexteram, tue cessent mine:
    Mediolanensium tante sunt ruine,
    quod in urbe media modo regnant spine.

24 Tantus erat populus atque locus ille:
    si venisset Gretia tota cum Achille,
    in qua tot sunt menia, tot potentes ville,
    non eam subicere possent annis mille.

25 Jussu tamen Cesaris obsidetur locus,
    donec ita venditur esca sicut crocus.
    In tanta penuria non est ibi iocus,
    ludum tandem Cesaris terminavit rocus.

26 Sonuit in auribus angulorum terre

When he came to contemplate the turmoil in the world   17
he embarked with vigour on a task to please the Lord;
to restore the kingdom to its former state, he called
on the cities to repay the taxes that they owed.

Pavia submitted to its master first of all: 18
a good city, flower of cities, famous, powerful, loyal;
it would have deserved my praise and a full description,
if my present way weren't that of practising concision.

After Pavia there stands next in line Novara,   19
for that city's sword waged war to defend the empire,
smashing and repelling with all its might and main
the aggressive action of arrogant Milan.

You shall live for ever, Novara, in my verse;   20
credit's due in every way to your citizens;
among the other cities, you'll be rich in praise
till the Alpine ranges are free from snow and ice.

So rejoice, Novara: you never shall grow old;   21
know that in my poems you shall be renewed;
there will be no day that brings an end to your renown;
after all your efforts, now peace is yours again.

The anguish of the Milanese people is enormous;   22
from excessive anguish they're scarcely in their senses;
the Ambrosian citizens are fierce with indignation
at being called upon, like slaves, to pay their contribution.

In the meantime, Constantine, hear me and be warned: 23
let your threats be ended now; lower your right hand;
such a state of ruin exists now in Milan
that in the city centre prickly bushes reign.

So great was the place itself and its population,   24
if Achilles had arrived with the whole Greek nation,
where there were so many walls, so many powerful villas,
they couldn't overcome it in a thousand years.

All the same, it was besieged at Frederick's injunction   25
till the price of meat became as high as that of saffron.
Such enormous poverty isn't any joke;
Caesar brought the game at last to checkmate with his rook.

News of this campaign was heard sounding in men's ears   26

et in maris insulis huius fama gerre;
quam si mihi liceat plenius referre,
hoc opus Eneidi poteris preferre.

27   Modis mille scriberem bellicos conflictus,
hostiles insidias et viriles ictus,
quantis minis impetit ensis hostem strictus,
qualiter progreditur castris rex invictus.

28   Erant in Ytalia greges vispillonum,
semitas obsederat rabies predonum,
quorum cor ad scelera semper erat pronum,
quibus malum facere videbatur bonum.

29   Cesaris est gloria, Cesaris est donum,
quod iam patent omnibus vie regionum,
dum ventis exposita corpora latronum
surda flantis boree captant aure sonum.

30   Iterum describitur orbis ab Augusto,
redditur res publica statui vetusto,
pax terras ingreditur habitu venusto,
et iam non opprimitur iustus ab iniusto.

31   Volat fama Cesaris velut velox ecus,
hac audita trepidat imperator Grecus;
iam quid agat nescius, iam timore cecus,
timet nomen Cesaris, ut leonem pecus.

32   Iam tiranno Siculo Siculi detrectant,
Siculi te siciunt, Cesar, et expectant,
iam libenter Apuli tibi genu flectant,
mirantur, quid detinet, oculos humectant.

33   Archicancellarius viam preparavit,
dilatavit semitas, vepres extirpavit;
ipse iugo Cesaris terram subiugavit
et me de miserie lacu liberavit.

34   Imperator nobilis, age sicut agis,
sicut exaltatus es, exaltare magis,
fove tuos subditos, hostes cede plagis,
super eos irruens ultione stragis.

26,2 *gerra* = Fr. *guerre*.   31,1 *ecus* = cl *equus.*

in the corners of the earth, the islands of the seas;
if I were permitted to give it more extended
treatment, you might well prefer this work to the Aeneid.

I'd describe the armed engagements in a thousand ways –   27
hostile tricks of strategy, valorous forays,
with what threats the naked sword struck at the assailant,
how the undefeated king advanced from his encampment.

Gangs of bandits, in the past, infested Italy;   28
by the roads they lay in wait, in their lust for booty;
their hearts were always ready to commit what crimes they could;
doing evil seemed to them the same as doing good.

Caesar's is the glory, though, and this gift is Caesar's,   29
that the region's roads are now open to all users,
while the robbers' corpses, exposed out in the winds,
catch in ears now deaf to it the blowing north wind's sound.

Once again Augustus makes a census of the world.   30
The state's returned to the condition it was in of old;
peace is entering our lands, beautifully dressed;
the just man is no longer oppressed by the unjust.

Caesar's reputation flies on like a swift horse;   31
the Byzantine emperor trembles at the news;
now, not knowing what to do, blinded by alarm,
just as cattle fear a lion he fears Caesar's name.

Sicily's rejecting now its tyrant's domination;   32
the Sicilians thirst for you, Caesar, in expectation;
now, too, the Apulians freely kneel to praise you;
tears are in their eyes as they wonder what delays you.

Your Archchancellor went first to prepare your way,   33
straightening the paths for you, clearing briars away;
he himself subdued the land under Caesar's yoke,
and has rescued me from my wretchedness's lake.

Noble emperor, persist in doing what you've started;   34
just as you're exalted now, you should be more exalted;
treat your subjects kindly, deal harshly with your foes,
crush them under the attack of your avenging blows.

X

1 Estuans intrinsecus ira vehementi
  in amaritudine loquor mee menti:
  factus de materia levis elementi
  folio sum similis de quo ludunt venti.

2 Cum sit enim proprium viro sapienti
  supra petram ponere sedem fundamenti,
  stultus ego comparor fluvio labenti
  sub eodem aere nunquam permanenti.

3 Feror ego veluti sine nauta navis,
  ut per vias aeris vaga fertur avis.
  Non me tenent vincula, non me tenet clavis,
  quero mei similes et adiungor pravis.

4 Mihi cordis gravitas res videtur gravis,
  iocus est amabilis dulciorque favis.
  Quidquid Venus imperat, labor est suavis,
  que nunquam in cordibus habitat ignavis.

5 Via lata gradior more iuventutis,
  inplico me viciis immemor virtutis,
  voluptatis avidus magis quam salutis,
  mortuus in anima curam gero cutis.

6 Presul discretissime, veniam te precor:
  morte bona morior, dulce nece necor,
  meum pectus sauciat puellarum decor,
  et quas tactu nequeo, saltem corde mechor.

7 Res est arduissima vincere naturam,
  in aspectu virginis mentem esse puram;
  iuvenes non possumus legem sequi duram
  leviumque corporum non habere curam.

8 Quis in igne positus igne non uratur?
  Quis Papie demorans castus habeatur,
  ubi Venus digito iuvenes venatur,
  oculis illaqueat, facie predatur?

Verbally my text follows Manitius, but I have altered some punctuation; in particular, I have chosen not to begin every line with a capital letter as he does.

X

Deep inside me I'm ablaze with an angry passion;   1
in my bitterness of mind, this is my confession:
I'm constructed out of some light and weightless matter
like a leaf, an idle toy for the winds to flutter.

After all, a man of sense, one with penetration,   2
builds his house upon a rock with a sure foundation.
I, however (what a fool!) wander like a river
never staying anywhere, on the move for ever.

I'm a drifting boat with no mariner to steer,   3
like an aimless bird that flies through the paths of air.
Nothing serves to hold me back, neither locks nor shackles,
when I seek bad company, looking for my equals.

Heavy-heartedness to me seems a heavy burden;   4
entertainment sweeter than honey's what I dote on.
Such commands as Venus gives make for easy working;
she is never found in hearts which go in for shirking.

Walking on the broader path, as a young man tends to,   5
I'm caught up in vices, and negligent of virtue.
Pleasure has me in its thrall, rather than salvation;
dead of soul, I care about physical sensation.

Wise and just archbishop, I ask for your forgiveness: 6
it's a lovely death I die, killed by fatal sweetness.
Female beauty wounds my breast; but if I can't win her
I commit adultery in my heart upon her.

It's the hardest thing of all to defeat your nature;   7
when you see a girl, to stay pure in mind is torture.
As young men we can't obey such a harsh injunction,
or ignore the silky-soft female form's attraction.

Who can walk through fire and be safe from conflagration? 8
In Pavia, who can stay pure in reputation?
Venus preys on young men here, lures them with a gesture,
snares them with a glancing eye or a pretty feature.

9 Si ponas Ypolitum hodie Papie,
  non erit Ypolitus in sequenti die:
  Veneris in thalamos ducunt omnes vie,
  non est in tot turribus turris Alethie.

10 Secundo redarguor etiam de ludo,
   sed cum ludus corpore me dimittat nudo,
   frigidus exterius, mentis estu sudo;
   tunc versus et carmina meliora cudo.

11 Tercio capitulo memoro tabernam:
   illam nullo tempore sprevi neque spernam,
   donec sanctos angelos venientes cernam,
   cantantes pro mortuis 'Requiem eternam'.

12 Meum est propositum in taberna mori,
   ut sint vina proxima morientis ori.
   Tunc cantabunt letius angelorum chori:
   'Sit deus propitius huic potatori'.

13 Poculis accenditur animi lucerna;
   cor inbutum nectare volat ad superna.
   Mihi sapit dulcius vinum de taberna
   quam quod aqua miscuit presulis pincerna.

14 Loca vitant publica quidam poetarum
   et secretas eligunt sedes latebrarum:
   student instant vigilant nec laborant parum,
   et vix tandem reddere possunt opus clarum.

15 Jeiunant et abstinent poetarum chori,
   vitant rixas publicas et tumultus fori,
   et, ut opus faciant quod non possit mori,
   moriuntur studio subditi labore.

16 Unicuique proprium dat natura munus:
   ego nunquam potui scribere ieiunus:
   me ieiunum vincere posset puer unus.
   Sitim et ieiunium odi tanquam funus.

17 Unicuique proprium dat natura donum.
   Ego versus faciens bibo vinum bonum,

15.3 *possit* Ma., *possint* Wa.

If you put Hippolytus in Pavia today,   9
he won't be Hippolytus when a night's gone by.
Every alley leads you to Venus and her boudoir;
in a place where towers are so many, Truth has no tower.

Secondly I stand accused of the sin of gambling;   10
but when I have diced away every stitch of clothing
mentally I seethe with heat, cold though my outside is;
at such times I hammer out better songs and verses.

Thirdly in this catalogue let me list the tavern.   11
I shall never spurn a pub (and I never have done),
till I see the heavenly host coming; till I hear it
singing 'Rest eternal' to each departed spirit.

In a tavern's where I'll die – so I have decided;   12
there my dying mouth and wine needn't be divided.
Then the choirs of angels will joyfully be singing
'God have mercy on this man who was always drinking.'

Cups of liquor make my soul light up like a lantern;   13
when the nectar soaks my heart, up it flies to heaven.
I prefer the tavern's wine: that, to me, is sweeter,
than the stuff that's watered down by a bishop's butler.

Certain poets tend to shun places that are public   14
and secrete themselves away somewhere claustrophobic;
sleeplessly they toil and strive; yet, for all their grinding,
seldom manage to produce anything outstanding.

Fasting and teetotal, these choirs of singing poets   15
keep away from public strife and the market's tumults;
in their efforts to compose works which live for ever
they expire in the attempt out of sheer endeavour.

Nature has made each of us idiosyncratic: 16
I could never write a word with an empty stomach;
any child could knock me down when I haven't eaten;
thirst and hunger are to me hateful as extinction.

Each of us, by nature, is given some advantage.   17
When I'm writing verse I drink wine of decent vintage

et quod habent purius dolia cauponum;
tale vinum generat copiam sermonum.

18   Tales versus facio, quale vinum bibo,
nihil possum facere nisi sumpto cibo;
nihil valent penitus, que ieiunus scribo;
Nasonem post calices carmine preibo.

19   Mihi nunquam spiritus poetrie datur,
nisi prius fuerit venter bene satur;
dum in arce cerebri Bachus dominatur,
in me Phebus irruit et miranda fatur.

20   Ecce mee proditor pravitatis fui,
de qua me redarguunt servientes tui.
Sed eorum nullus est accusator sui,
quamvis velint ludere seculoque frui.

21   Jam nunc in presentia presulis beati
secundum dominici regulam mandati
mittat in me lapidem neque parcat vati,
cuius non est animus conscius peccati.

22   Sum locutus contra me, quicquid de me novi,
et virus evomui, quod tam diu fovi.
Vita vetus displicet, mores placent novi;
homo videt faciem, sed cor patet Iovi.

23   Iam virtutes diligo, viciis irascor,
renovatus animo spiritu renascor;
quasi modo genitus novo lacte pascor,
ne sit meum amplius vanitatis vas cor.

24   Electe Colonie, parce penitenti,
fac misericordiam veniam petenti,
et da penitenciam culpam confitenti:
feram quicquid iusseris animo libenti.

25   Parcit enim subditis leo rex ferarum
et est erga subditos immemor irarum;
et vos idem facite, principes terrarum:
quod caret dulcedine, nimis est amarum.

19,1 Some MSS have *prophetie*, as in poem IV, 15,1
26–30 In the Codex Buranus five extra strophes, probably not by the Archpoet, are added:
see the following Appendix.

and the best that's to be found in the landlord's pantry;
wine like that will generate rhetoric in plenty.

How I write is governed by the kind of wine I swallow;   18
poetry's impossible when my stomach's hollow;
what I write when fasting is feeble and insipid;
when I've had a glass or two I can outsing Ovid.

I am never given poetic inspiration   19
if my stomach isn't first sated to repletion;
but when Bacchus holds his sway in my mental fortress,
Phoebus rushes into me and pronounces wonders.

There: I've spoken out about all that's on my conscience,   20
answering the charges brought by your Lordship's servants.
None of those, however, has made his own confession,
much though they may revel in dice and dissipation.

Now in the most reverend Lord Archbishop's presence,   21
following the precepts of Holy Writ for guidance,
if a stone is due to be cast against the poet,
let the man that's without sin be the first to throw it.

I've declared against myself all I know that's wrong,   22
spewing out the poison I harboured for so long.
Now I want new habits; my former life offends me;
men go by appearances: Jove can see inside me.

Now I love the virtues; the vices rouse my wrath;   23
I'm renewed in mind, with a spiritual rebirth;
like a newborn baby I'm drinking milk that's fresh,
so my mind will cease to be filled with worthless trash.

Archbishop-elect, be kind to me in my contrition;   24
since I ask forgiveness, please treat me with compassion;
now that I've confessed to my guilt for how I've sinned,
I'll do penance gladly, whatever you command.

After all, the lion, king over the wild creatures,   25
treats his subjects tenderly, sparing them his rages.
Do the same, you princes who rule as earthly kings;
that which has no sweetness is a far too bitter thing.

Appendix to poem x

26 Cum sit fama multiplex de te divulgata,
    veritati consonent omnia prolata;
    colorare stultum est bene colorata,
    et non decet aliquem serere iam sata.

27 Raptus ergo specie fame decurrentis
    veni non inmodicum verba dare ventis,
    sed ut rorem gratie de profundo mentis,
    ut precepit dominus, traham offerentis.

28 Vide, si complaceat tibi me tenere;
    in scribendis litteris certus sum valere,
    et si forsan accidat opus imminere,
    vices in dictamine potero supplere.

29 Hoc si recusaveris, audi quod attendas:
    paupertatis oneri pie condescendas
    et ad penas hominis huius depellendas
    curam aliquantenus muneris impendas.

30 Pater mi, sub brevi tam multa comprehendi;
    quia doctis decus est modus hic loquendi,
    et ut prorsus resecem notam applaudendi,
    non in verba lacius placuit protendi.

Appendix to poem x

Many-faceted although your fame is, and widespread,   26
there shall be accord with truth in everything that's said;
it's foolish to add colours to something nicely coloured,
and wrong for anyone to sow ground already seeded.

Ravished, therefore, by the charm of your abundant fame,   27
it's not to give words wildly to the winds that I have come,
but to bring the dew of thanks, out of the profound
regions of the giver's heart, as was our Lord's command.

Look: if it should please you to keep me in employment,   28
as a letter-writer I'm sure to be efficient;
and if it should come about that some work turns up
in composition I shall be fit to fill the gap.

But if you refuse this, hear what you should attend to: 29
the burden of my poverty you should kindly bend to,
and so that this man's poverty may be sent away,
you should spend a little care on a gift for me.

Father, so much is contained in so short a span,   30
for such a way of speaking suits educated men,
and in order to avoid the charge of overpraise
this is where I choose to stop, with no more words than these.

Explanatory notes

Poem I

1 In my version of this poem I am indebted to that of Peter Dronke (see 'The art of the Archpoet: a reading of "Lingua balbus"' in *The Interpretation of Medieval Lyric Poetry*, 1980).

3,2 See Matthew 5,15.

4,4 *Tu autem*: see note on Primas 4,15.

10,4 See Matthew 24,24.

13,2 See Matthew 7,14.

14,1 See Proverbs 24,12.

15,2 See Eccl. 1,2.

27,1 See Matthew 25, 1–13.

32 See Matthew 19, 23ff.; I Cor. 13,13; Cicero 'De Officiis' III, vi,28.

33,2 I follow Dronke's interpretation.

39 St Martin gave half a cloak to a beggar (but it was his own cloak, which the poet here ignores, to make his patron sound more generous).

41,1 *Vates* can mean 'poet' or 'prophet'; usually the former is more apt when the Archpoet refers to himself, but here there is also a reference to the story of Elijah, to whom the widow gave the last of her oil (see I Kings 17). See also str. 44.

44 'Eloy' echoes the name by which Christ, in his agony on the cross, called on God, and people in the crowd exclaimed that he was calling Elijah (Matthew 27, 46–7; Mark 15,35–6). The cruse of oil also occurred in the story of Elijah. The Archpoet here identifies it with the 'oil of charity' in str. 27.

Poem II

1 In this poem, based on the book of Jonah, the poet uses events from the biblical narrative as humorous parallels for his own plight. Jonah fled from the

wrath of God at Nineveh, was thrown overboard and swallowed by a 'great fish'. Just so the poet has fled from his patron, the Archchancellor Rainald, and been swallowed up by poverty. The poem is addressed to Rainald, and was probably written in 1164.

5–6 *Vienna*: Vienne in Burgundy.

7 *marchionum*: these were the Burgundian lords: *marchio* is a title of nobility, used here in a general sense for the sake of alliteration.

11 *diem nonum*: the Nones of the month.

35 See Jonah 1,7.

41–2 Paraphrasing Matthew 26,41 and Mark 14,38.

47,49 These refer to the poet's present poverty and hunger.

56 The dual meaning of '*vates*' – 'prophet' and 'poet', embracing both Jonah and the poet – is lost in English. In medieval paintings Jonah was depicted as bald and naked, like a newborn baby, when the whale had spewed him out. Presumably the Archpoet was himself bald, but there is also a spiritual suggestion of new life and purification here.

70 See Jonah 1,3.

94 See John 15,5.

Poem III

1 The poem is in hexameters, all but the first two lines with Leonine rhyme. The layout of the Latin text, highlighting final letters, is not suited to the English version, where it is more helpful to show the line-breaks at the caesura.

1 See Eccl. 3,1.

19 The poet may have been genuinely ill, but more probably this is humorous exaggeration.

Poem IV

1 Rainald has asked the Archpoet to write an epic praising the achievements of the Emperor.

4 Some editors see this and the following strophe as two attempts at the same subject-matter; Langosch omits this one. But they are more probably intentional variations on the theme (like the *laisses parallèles* in chansons de geste, as P. Dronke notes).

7,1 See Jeremiah 10,23.

9,1 See Horace, *Ars P.* 390 and *Epist.* 1,18,71.

10–15 These strophes occur again in Poem x, 14–19, where they have a slightly different function. They seem originally to have been composed for IV, however, and offer a basis for the poet's refusal of Rainald's commission.

10 The idea that poets prefer solitude was common in classical times; see Horace, *Ars P.* 298.

12,1 See Propertius 2.22, 17ff. and I Cor. 7,7; the Archpoet combines echoes from both sources. (See Dronke, 'The Archpoet and the Classics', p. 66, on this whole passage).

12,4 For the Archpoet thirst is more serious than hunger.

13–14 See Horace, *Epist.* 1,5,19ff. and 1,19,2–8.

16,2–3 *Latium* and *Tuscus* in a general sense for 'Italy' and 'Italian'.

16,4 *Preter te* = 'except you'. Manitius took this as 'I can do nothing without your help.' Watenphul & Krefeld, however, agree with Langosch that the Archpoet means 'I can praise no one but you.'

18,1 This line and 19,1 make up a quotation from Luke 16,3: 'I cannot dig; to beg I am ashamed.' As a scholar of noble birth (*ortus ex militibus*) the Archpoet was not incapable of digging, but merely above it: his family came from a higher class.

19,1 To ask in verse for presents was not regarded as begging.

20,1 *Viri litterati* are the clerics: men of academic education (including bishops), in contrast to the *laici*.

22,2 See Ephesians 5,5, where a covetous man is described as an idolater.

24,1 The knights are the *laici* of 20,3.

25,3 These are the 'parasites' of 23,1.

26,2 See note on 22,2.

27,1–2 The play on words connects *Reginaldus* with *regnum*.

28,3 *Vellus* could be a fleece, or a lining for a coat. See Primas, Poem 2.

30 See Poem I, 31,1: even the poor had a duty to give alms to those who were poorer. The Archpoet has cunningly directed his charity towards having prayers said for Rainald's success in Italy.

32,3 Manitius explains this as meaning that to do so would be to risk losing his independence.

Poem v

1 The poem makes humorous use of the 'Vision' genre. It must have been written in the second half of 1164; Watenphul & Krefeld suggest two possible dates: the festival of St Martin (11 Nov.) or All Saints' Day (1 Nov.) The situation is not now easy to reconstruct in detail. The Archpoet had been living for some time in the monastery of St Martin, in Cologne; Rainald, to whom the poem is addressed, was also in Cologne.

1,1 '*Nox sabbati*' was the night preceding the Sabbath: i.e. the early hours of Sunday morning.

2,2 Visions traditionally began with exotic odours and brilliant light.

7 Aristotle and Homer, who belonged to the pagan world, are absent, but St Augustine, who throughout the Middle Ages was thought to have written a Latin version of Aristotle's *Categories*, is present.

12,2 See Matthew 3,10.

12,3 William I of Sicily.

14,1 St Martin.

14,4 *dicit* is in the present tense because St Martin is still expressing his anger at the time of the poem's writing.

19,1–2 A humorous touch: it is the monastery, not the saint in person, which has provided the poet with wine.

19,3 The Count Palatine at this time was Konrad, Frederick's half-brother.

21 Humorous exaggeration.

22 A person on his deathbed ought to forgive his enemies.

24 The Vulgate's version of Psalm 22 (Ps. 23 in the AV) begins 'Dominus regit me et nihil me deerit: in loco pascuae ibi me collocavit.' This whole strophe plays on the words of the psalm. There is a pun on the two meanings of *claustrum*: 'sheepfold' and 'cloister'. The abbot is 'the good shepherd' (see John 10,11 and 14).

Poem VI

1 The poem changes its form halfway through: Leonine hexameters to line 22, then five quatrains with end-rhymes.

8 The illness was probably malaria, which was common in southern Italy in the Middle Ages.

18 *nudus* is an instance of the Archpoet's customary exaggeration.

28 See II Cor. 9,7.

33 There is disagreement as to whether the poem was written in Italy or Germany. Manitius takes *trans Alpes* as Italy, *hic* as Cologne. Watenphul & Krefeld incline to the opinion that *trans Alpes* = in Germany, *hic* northern Italy. My rendering leaves the question open.

36 This refers to the Italians.

37 See Matthew 6,20.

Poem VII

1 The poem was written for All Saint's Day; Watenphul & Krefeld suggest that the year was 1162.

14 See Matthew 10,16.

18 See note to Poem 1,39.

22 Milan fell to Frederick's army in March 1162.

32 Irus was a beggar in the *Odyssey*, 18,239.

33 The melody has been laid over the text like a cloak over a tunic. ·

Poem VIII

1 Cologne was originally named Colonia Agrippinae, after Agrippina, Nero's mother.

Poem IX

1,2   See Matthew 11,30.

1,3   See Acts 9,5 and 26,14.

1,4   See Acts 7,51.

2,2   This refers to the taking of Milan and other cities, and plays with the image of the fall of Jericho at the sound of the trumpet; see Joshua 6,5.

4,1   A humorous link with the preceding line.

4,2   See Matthew 22,17.

4,3   See Mark 12,42.

8,2   The 'anointed lord' is here the Emperor, not Christ; the wordplay on *Christo* is lost in English.

9,2   See Isaiah 34,13 and also Primas, Poem 9.

10   See Genesis 11,4.

10,3   See Vergil, *Georgics* IV,170.

12,3   St Ambrose had been bishop of Milan.

13,3   'the fates': *fatis* is plural for the sake of the rhyme, but the meaning is, in effect, 'God', who governs people's fates.

14,3   See I Maccabaeus 3,1.

17,2   i.e. the task of restoring order to the world of Christendom.

18,1   Pavia had been capital of the Lombard kingdom before Milan was, and had remained loyal to Frederick.

18,2   *pia* is not to be taken literally as referring to moral virtue, but rather to the city's dutiful attitude to the Emperor; cf. Poem X, 8ff. The Pavia of that poem might not have recognised itself in the present description.

19,1   Watenphul & Krefeld suggest, in view of the praise given to Novara, that the poem may have been recited before the Emperor there.

21,1   An echo of 'Laetare, Jerusalem' (Introit to the Mass for the 4th Sunday in Lent).

21,1–2   There is a pun on *Novaria/renovari*.

23,1   Constantine: a traditional designation for the Byzantine emperor – at that time Manuel, who supported Milan.

24   A reference to the Trojan War, which lasted ten years; the Archpoet's hyperbole claims that even a thousand would not suffice in this case.

25,4   The rook in chess has the form of a castle; the punning reference is to the siege-tower used in battle.

28,1   'bandits': *vispillones* are lit. thieves who robbed corpses.

29,3   'exposed': i.e. hanging on the branches of trees.

29,4   Manitius suggests that the north wind was perhaps chosen because it blew from the direction of Germany.

30,1   See Luke 2,1. The AV translates '. .a decree from Caesar Augustus that all the world should be taxed.' The NEB has '. .for a registration to be made. . .' The assessment or census is part of the new world order being imposed by Frederick.

31   The Byzantine emperor could also claim to be called 'Caesar', but the Archpoet's rhetoric implicitly rejects this claim.

32,1 The 'Tyrant' of Sicily was William I, recognised as king by Pope Hadrian in 1156.

32,3 Apulia was also part of William's Norman kingdom.

33,1–2 See Mark 1,2–3; Matthew 11,10; Luke 7,27; the Archchancellor performed the function of John the Baptist.

Poem x

1 This well-known poem appears in a great many manuscripts, and with a number of minor variations. As early as the 13th c. it was known as the 'Confession'.

1,1–2 These lines contain biblical echoes from Genesis 6,6 and Job 10,1 (and *vehementi* may echo Genesis 27,33 or 50,10).

2,1–2 See Matthew 7,24.

5 See Matthew 7,13.

6 See Matthew 5,28.

8,3–4 Lit. 'where Venus hunts young men with a [beckoning] finger, ensnares them with her eyes, preys on them with her looks.'.

9,1–2 Hippolytus was famous for his chastity when tempted by his stepmother Phaedra: see Vergil *Aen.* VII, 761ff. and Ovid *Met.* XV, 487ff.

9,4 Alethia (lit. 'Truth') is used here, for the sake of the rhyme, in place of the Christian concept of Virtue.

14–19 These six strophes are repeated from Poem IV,10–15.

20,1–2 He returns to the charges laid against him (cf. str. 10,1) and turns them against his accusers.

21,3–4 See John 8,7.

22,4 'Jove' for 'God', for the sake of the rhyme.

24 Lit. 'you who are the [Archbishop] elect of Cologne'. Rainald long delayed his acceptance of the office of Archbishop, because he preferred imperial politics to pastoral duties.

Bibliographical note

The relevant texts of the two poets are as follows:

Meyer, W. *Die Oxforder Gedichte des Primas (des Magisters Hugo von Orléans)*, Nachrichten von der königlichen Gesellschaft der Wissenschaften zu Göttingen, phil.-hist. Klasse 1907, Heft 1, s.75–111; Heft 2, s.113–75,231–4 (Berlin, 1907; repr. Darmstadt, 1970).

McDonough, C. J. *The Oxford Poems of Hugh Primas and the Arundel Lyrics* (Toronto, 1984).

Manitius, M. *Die Gedichte des Archipoeta* (Munich, 1916; 2nd edn 1929).

Watenphul, H. and Krefeld, H. *Die Gedichte des Archipoeta* (Heidelberg, 1958).

Langosch, K. *Hymnen und Vagantenlieder* (Basel, 1954).

My texts are based on those of Meyer, for Hugh Primas, and Manitius (1929) for the Archpoet, but I have also referred to and sometimes been guided by the others. In particular I should note that Manitius introduced a new system of numbering the poems of the Archpoet, which has caused subsequent confusion. (Langosch adopted yet another system). I have reverted, following Watenphul and Krefeld, to the original system of Jakob Grimm (Akad. Wiss. Berlin 1843, = Kleinere Schriften III, Berlin, 1866).

My textual notes are on the whole restricted to instances in which I have diverged from the texts of Meyer and Manitius. For full textual notes the reader is referred to the editions above.

I have used the following abbreviations or sigla for the editions and manuscripts:

R   Oxford Bodleian MS Rawlinson G 109
B   Berlin theol. lat. Oct. 94
C   Paris BN lat. 18570
H   London BL Harley 978
P   Paris BN lat. 16208
Ma   Manitius

Wa   Watenphul and Krefeld
Br   Brussels Bibl. Royale 2076
Go   Univ. Bibl. Göttingen Cod. philol.170

In addition to the editions of the poets, I have found the following books and articles useful:

Curtius, E. R. 'Die Musen im Mittelalter', *Zeitschrift für romanische Philologie* 59 (1939) 129–88.

Dronke, P. 'The Archpoet and the Classics', *Latin Poetry and the Classical Tradition: Essays in Medieval and Renaissance Literature*, edn P. Godman and O. Murray (Oxford, 1990) 57–72.

'The Art of the Archpoet: a Reading of "Lingua Balbus"', *The Interpretation of Medieval Lyric Poetry*, ed. W. T. H. Jackson (New York, 1980) 22–43.

The Medieval Lyric, 2nd edn (Cambridge, 1977).

'The Return of Eurydice', *Classica et mediaevalia* 23 (1962) 198–215.

Ehlers, W.-W. 'Zum 16. Gedicht des Hugo von Orléans', *Mittellateinisches Jahrbuch* 12 (1977) 78–81.

Jackson, W. T. H. 'The Politics of a Poet: the Archipoeta as Revealed by his Imagery', *Philosophy and Humanism: Renaissance Essays in Honor of Paul Oskar Kristeller*, ed. P. Mahoney (Leiden, 1976) 320–38.

Kate, R. Ten. 'Hugo Primas XXXIII: Dives eram et dilectus' *Classica et mediaevalia* 25 (1964) 205–14.

Latzke, T. 'Der Topos Mantelgedicht', *Mittellateinisches Jahrbuch* 6 (1970) 109–31.

McDonough, C. J. 'Miscellaneous Notes to Hugo Primas and Arundel 1', *Mittellateinishes Jahrbuch* 14 (1979) 187–99.

'Two Poems of Hugh Primas Reconsidered: 18 and 23', *Traditio* 39 (1983) 133–55.

Mann, Jill. 'Satiric Subject and Satiric Object in Goliardic Literature', *Mittellateinisches Jahrbuch* 15 (1980) 63–86.

Marti, B. M. 'Hugh Primas and Arnulf of Orléans', *Speculum* 30 (1955) 233–8.

Raby, F. J. E. *A History of Secular Latin Poetry in the Middle Ages*. 2v. (Oxford, 1934).

Rigg, A. G. 'Golias and Other Pseudonyms', *Studi medievali* 3rd s.18 (1977) 65–109.

Williams, J. R. 'The Cathedral School of Reims in the Time of Master Alberic, 1118–1136', *Traditio* 20 (1964) 93–114.